THE
NBA'S
GREATEST
PLAYERS

JOHN FAWAZ

Whitman
Publishing, LLC
PUBLISHING SINCE 1934

www.whitman.com

The NBA's Greatest Players

www.whitman.com
© 2012 Whitman Publishing, LLC

Excluding certain works, whose copyright may or may not be noted, ©2012 Whitman Publishing, LLC
3101 Clairmont Road · Suite G · Atlanta GA 30329

Correspondence concerning this book may be directed to the publisher, at the address above.

ISBN: 0794837646
Printed and assembled in China

To view other products from Whitman Publishing, please visit Whitman.com.

Scan the QR code above to browse
Whitman Publishing's full selection
of sports and specialty books.

TABLE OF CONTENTS

THE COMPETITIVE GREATNESS

By John Fawaz

The court is the same size, the rim is the same height and the objective is the same — put the ball into the hoop. Everything else has changed since the NBA made its debut in 1946.

Well, *almost* everything. Great players still dominate, more so in basketball than in any other team sport. Which is not to say that one player alone can win a championship. A basketball team is a group of players trying to perform in harmony, but like any ensemble, a virtuoso can elevate the group.

The NBA's virtuosos can be found in the pages that follow. Some are obvious, such as Michael Jordan, whose exploits transcended the game and made him a global icon. Others are not so well known, such as Paul Arizin, one of the first jump shooters. Many were superstars during their time, and others were not fully appreciated until much later.

The 75 players featured in this book are a diverse lot, incorporating many different styles and contributing to their teams in ways not always reflected in box scores. But all have left an imprint — or are making an imprint — on the sport. These are the NBA's royalty, a line that can be traced from George Mikan all the way to today's king, LeBron James. Mikan and James are dramatically different, yet they share certain innate qualities, as do all of the NBA's greatest players.

"I've asked some of the older coaches, 'What made the players of earlier eras great? What separated them from all the others?'" said Bill Walton, who was selected as one of the NBA's 50 Greatest Players in 1996 (all 50 are included in this book). "And it is the same simple answer that makes players excel today — heart, brains, soul and competitive greatness."

That competitive greatness continues to drive the NBA's evolution. Uneasy lies the crown, as James finds himself challenged by a crop of younger players, led by Kevin Durant. That, too, is a part of the game that has not changed, and never will.

IN VERY GOOD HANDS

Growing up in Louisiana, I admired a pair of players from the state who did great things in the NBA. My idol was Bill Russell. He was left-handed like me, and I wanted to block shots and play defense like him. He led the Celtics to so many titles, and I didn't win a championship until he finally retired. I liked what he brought to the game as a difference maker. I also liked St. Louis' Bob Pettit, who was a great scorer.

I was drafted by the Knicks in 1964 out of Grambling. Starting my pro career, the NBA was a much different world, as there were only nine teams. The Knicks drafted great players such as Walt "Clyde" Frazier along the way, and the club traded for Dave DeBusschere. Both of them were big parts of our two NBA titles in 1970 and 1973.

Clyde was a good team leader, a great rebounder, defensive player and scorer. DeBusschere was a power forward who could play on the perimeter, handle the ball and was one of the best long-range shooters in the NBA.

During my era, I was privileged to play against some of the greatest talents that the NBA ever had, many of whom you will read about in this book of *The NBA's Greatest Players*.

The greatest big man when I came into the league was Wilt Chamberlain. His ability to score, rebound and dominate the game made a big difference. My first game against Wilt, I was excited that I scored 32 points until I looked at the stats and saw that I "held" him to 56!

Kareem Abdul-Jabbar was a phenomenal player. Elvin Hayes, another Louisiana product, had one of the prettiest and toughest jump shots. I could not believe a player of Oscar Robertson's size could do all of the things he did as a rebounder, assist man and scorer. He and Elgin Baylor were ahead of their time. All of them had a profound impact on the game.

Other great players of my era include Jerry West, a tremendous competitor. We had some unbelievable battles against him and the Lakers in three NBA Finals. The Celtics' John Havlicek was a tremendous sixth man.

After I retired and moved into coaching and eventually front-office work, I enjoyed watching Bob Lanier, Moses Malone, Bill Walton, Magic Johnson, Larry Bird and Kevin McHale. The game continued to evolve with Michael Jordan, Hakeem Olajuwon, Dominique Wilkins, Karl Malone, Patrick Ewing, David Robinson, Tim Duncan, Kobe Bryant, Shaquille O'Neal and others too numerous to list.

I am still a big fan of the game. I watch the up-and-coming players, and what I see impresses me. The NBA has some good young talent such as LeBron James, Dirk Nowitzki, Kevin Durant and many more who really love the game of basketball. The game is in very good hands.

— Willis Reed,
New York Knicks, 1964-1974

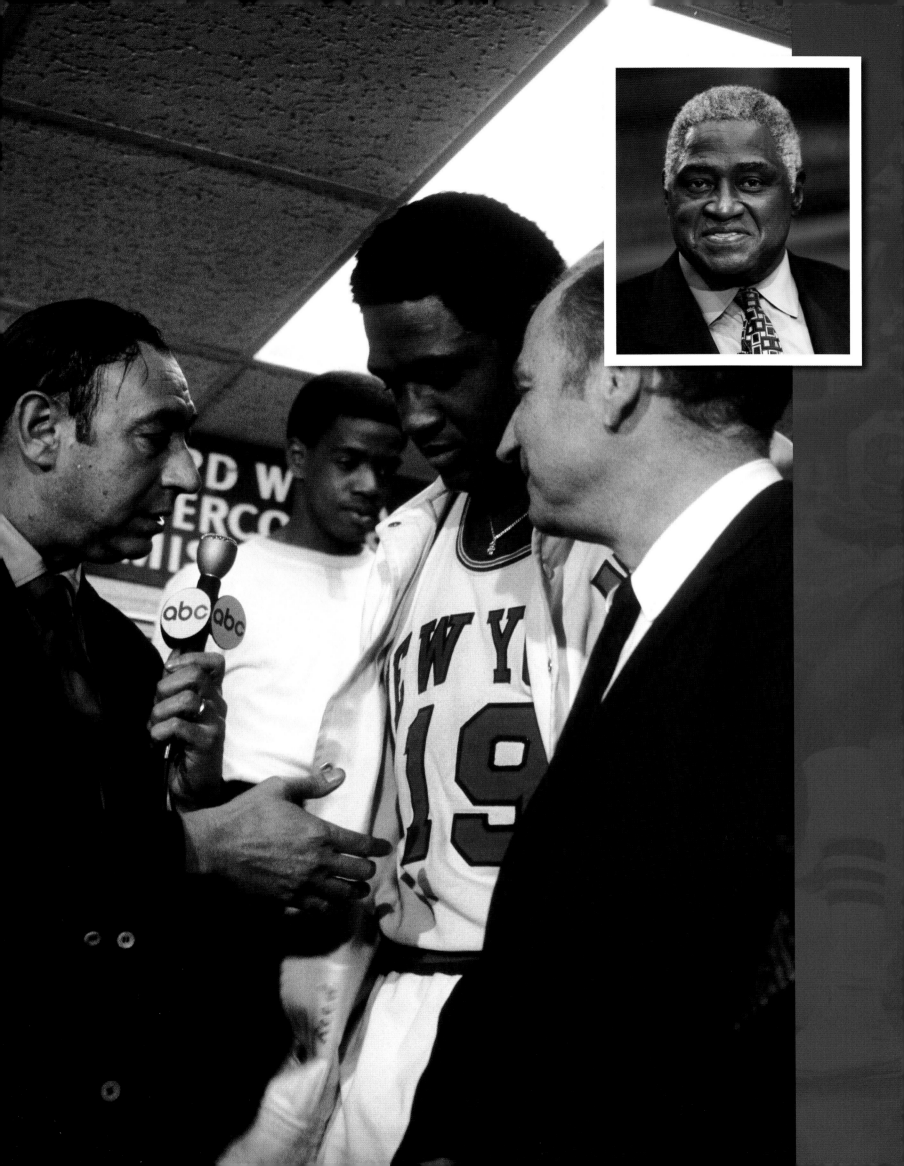

Earvin "Magic" Johnson once described Los Angeles Lakers teammate Kareem Abdul-Jabbar as "the most beautiful athlete in sport."

Such words are not normally associated with a 7-foot-2 center. Then again, Abdul-Jabbar was not your average 7-footer. He was a graceful giant who relied on brains more than brawn.

His signature shot — the skyhook — truly was a thing of beauty. Abdul-Jabbar, with his back to the basket, would fake right, pivot left and rise up, his left shoulder pointed at the basket. He would release the ball, which he held aloft in his fully extended right arm, with a seemingly effortless flick of the wrist. Unlike a traditional hook shot, Kareem's skyhook was impossible to block.

Abdul-Jabbar, then known by his birth name of Lew Alcindor, learned the shot in fifth grade. He already towered over his classmates at that age, so he played mostly against older, bigger kids. The skyhook, he says, "was the only shot that didn't get smashed back into my face." Thus, the most potent shot in basketball history was born.

Unparalleled success followed. Alcindor led Power Memorial High School to 71 consecutive victories and three straight New York City Catholic championships. He led UCLA to an 88-2 record and three NCAA titles in three seasons (NCAA rules barred freshmen from playing varsity basketball in those days).

Kareem Abdul-Jabbar, the name he adopted after converting to Islam at age 21, went on to play 20 seasons in the NBA — six with the Milwaukee Bucks and 14 with the Los Angeles Lakers. His résumé includes a record six NBA MVP Awards, six NBA championships and 38,387 points, the most in league history. Since his retirement in 1989, Abdul-Jabbar has coached young players, served as an NBA assistant and written several best-selling nonfiction books about African-American history.

All of the artistic and poetic metaphors have been used to describe Ray Allen's 3-point shot, and deservedly so. He rises up from the hardwood with his shoulders square to the basket, his right hand under the ball and his right elbow tucked underneath. Allen releases the ball at the top of his jump, with no wasted motion. The action is smooth and mesmerizing.

That shot is not only one of the most beautiful elements of the NBA game but also one of the most effective. Allen has made more 3-point baskets than any other player in NBA history, and he makes it look easy. But to paraphrase Thomas Edison, Allen's genius is one percent inspiration, 99 percent perspiration.

Allen shoots every day, 300 shots of all varieties on game day and many more on off days or during the offseason. The shots Allen attempts in games are just a fraction of the shots he has attempted in his lifetime. During games, Allen always has a defender attached to his hip. He overcomes such attention with remarkable conditioning, a quick release and a high basketball IQ.

Always a hard worker, Allen adopted his obsessive practice routine early in his NBA career, when he realized that athletic ability alone was not enough.

"I gotta do everything that I would do in a game because the court doesn't change. The only thing that changes is your defender," Allen recalled in a 2011 interview. "So I said, 'Every shot that I take in a game, potentially that I could take in every spot, I'm going to start practicing.'"

Allen, the fifth player selected in the 1996 NBA Draft, played in Milwaukee and Seattle before joining the Celtics in 2007. He scored 26 points in the decisive Game 6 of the 2008 NBA Finals to help Boston win its first title in 22 years.

No matter how tense the situation during the 2003 NCAA Tournament, Carmelo Anthony kept smiling. "I smile all the time," Anthony said when asked by a reporter. "Even when I'm in a bad mood, I try to keep a smile on my face."

Anthony's smile only grew after he led Syracuse to the national title that year. Though just a freshman, Anthony "was by far the best player in college basketball," said Syracuse coach Jim Boeheim. "It wasn't even close."

In the NBA, the 6-foot-8 Anthony is still at the head of the class, first in Denver and now in New York with the Knicks. Carmelo's complete offensive game makes him one of the league's top small forwards, an unstoppable force who averaged nearly 25 points per game during his first nine pro seasons.

Anthony is one of the most difficult players to cover one-on-one. He has an amazingly quick first step, allowing him to blow by most defenders, along with an array of spin moves. His post-up game and long arms allow him to overwhelm shorter players, and his deadly outside shooting forces opponents to defend him all over the court. Most importantly, Anthony can knock down shots with hands in his face and fingers tugging on his jersey.

"Carmelo…can make shots [against] good defense," said Celtics coach Doc Rivers. "That's what separates him. That's what makes him a great player."

Knicks fans hope Anthony's greatness will translate into a title. The hometown boy — Carmelo lived in Brooklyn until age 8 — returned to New York in February 2011 as part of a 13-player, three-team trade.

"I'm sitting here in one of the best places in the world," Anthony said. "It takes a certain kind of person to be able to do it in New York City and I'm willing to accept those challenges."

NATE "TINY" ARCHIBALD

For more than a decade, Nate "Tiny" Archibald weaved his way through the NBA's giants. Fans marveled at the quickness and fearlessness displayed by the 6-foot-1, 160-pound guard. As it turned out, 7-footers were the least of his obstacles.

Archibald, the oldest of seven children, grew up in a New York City neighborhood plagued by drugs and violence. Steering clear of such troubles became all the more difficult when his father left the family. Nate, a shy sophomore, contemplated dropping out of high school. He was struggling in class, had failed to make the varsity basketball team and his mom needed help at home.

Fortunately for all, he stayed in school. A basketball coach at a local community center convinced Archibald to work on his game and try out again next year. Teachers at the school helped him bring up his grades.

"They saw something in me I didn't see in myself," Archibald told a class of middle school students in 2002. "Today, I'm enjoying the benefits of their vision."

Archibald went on to earn a scholarship to the University of Texas at El Paso and play 13 seasons in the NBA. Early in his career, "Nate the Skate" scored in bunches, alternating between jump shots and explosive drives to the hoop. In 1972-73, his third year, he became the only person to lead the NBA in scoring (34.0 points per game) and assists (11.4) in the same season. He earned the first of his three All-NBA First Team selections that season.

Injuries slowed Archibald during the late 1970s and he became less of a scorer and more of a floor general. He played five seasons in Boston, leading the Celtics to the 1981 NBA title. After retiring in 1984, Archibald returned to New York to work with underprivileged children.

PAUL ARIZIN

Paul Arizin helped the NBA get off the ground — literally.

During the 1940s, basketball was a plodding game, with low scores and little movement. Two-handed set shots or one-handed hook shots, with one or both feet planted firmly on the hardwood, were the norm. Then the jump shot appeared, and though he wasn't the first, "Pitchin' Paul" was certainly one of the most proficient.

He mastered the jump shot almost by accident. Cut from his high school team, but still hooked on hoops, Arizin played whenever and wherever he could in his hometown of Philadelphia. The venues often were less than ideal.

"Some of our games were played on dance floors, [and] it became slippery," Arizin said. "When I tried to hook, my feet would go out from under me, so I jumped. I was always a good jumper. My feet weren't on the floor, so I didn't have to worry about slipping. The more I did it, the better I became."

Arizin's jump shot earned him a starting spot at nearby Villanova. He scored 25.3 points per game as a senior, at the time the second-highest average ever posted by a college player. Opponents found it difficult to corral the 6-foot-4 Arizin, whose athleticism and dribbling prowess allowed him to create open shots. Suddenly the game of basketball was in motion.

Arizin was no less unstoppable in the NBA. He played 10 seasons at forward for the hometown Philadelphia Warriors (he missed two seasons because of military service), retiring in 1962 as the third-leading scorer in NBA history (16,266 points). Arizin averaged 22.8 points per game during his career, earned 10 All-Star selections, and led the Warriors to the 1956 NBA title by scoring 28.9 points per game during that season's playoffs.

Before he became an outsized media personality, Charles Barkley was an outsized basketball player — and one of the best power forwards ever.

Initially, though, NBA teams didn't know what to make of Barkley. He possessed undeniable ability, but he seemingly lacked the height (he was generously listed at 6-foot-6) to play forward. Worries about his weight (his nickname was the "Round Mound of Rebound") and his work ethic added to the uncertainty.

But after Philadelphia selected Barkley in the 1984 NBA Draft, he quickly removed all doubt. Mentored by a veteran 76ers squad, the brash youngster became an All-Star by his third year. His power and determination made him one of the NBA's top rebounders, while his quickness and perimeter game allowed him to score inside and out. He played relentlessly from tipoff until the final buzzer.

"Sir Charles" proved to be even more entertaining off the court. A perennial member of the media-selected "All-Interview Team," his comments were funny, candid, insightful and often controversial, but never boring. He was a unique and colorful player who has gone on to become a unique, colorful and hugely popular presence on television.

When Barkley retired in 2000, he was one of only four NBA players to have amassed 20,000 points, 10,000 rebounds and 4,000 assists. His 16 seasons were divided among Philadelphia (1984-1992), Phoenix (1992-1996) and Houston (1996-2000). He finished with career averages of 22.1 points and 11.7 rebounds per game, five All-NBA First Team selections and the 1992-93 NBA MVP Award. He also helped the U.S. win Olympic gold medals in 1992 and 1996, leading the "Dream Team" in scoring each time.

"There is nobody who does what Barkley does," said Hall of Fame center Bill Walton. "He's a dominant rebounder, a dominant defensive player, a 3-point shooter, a dribbler, a playmaker."

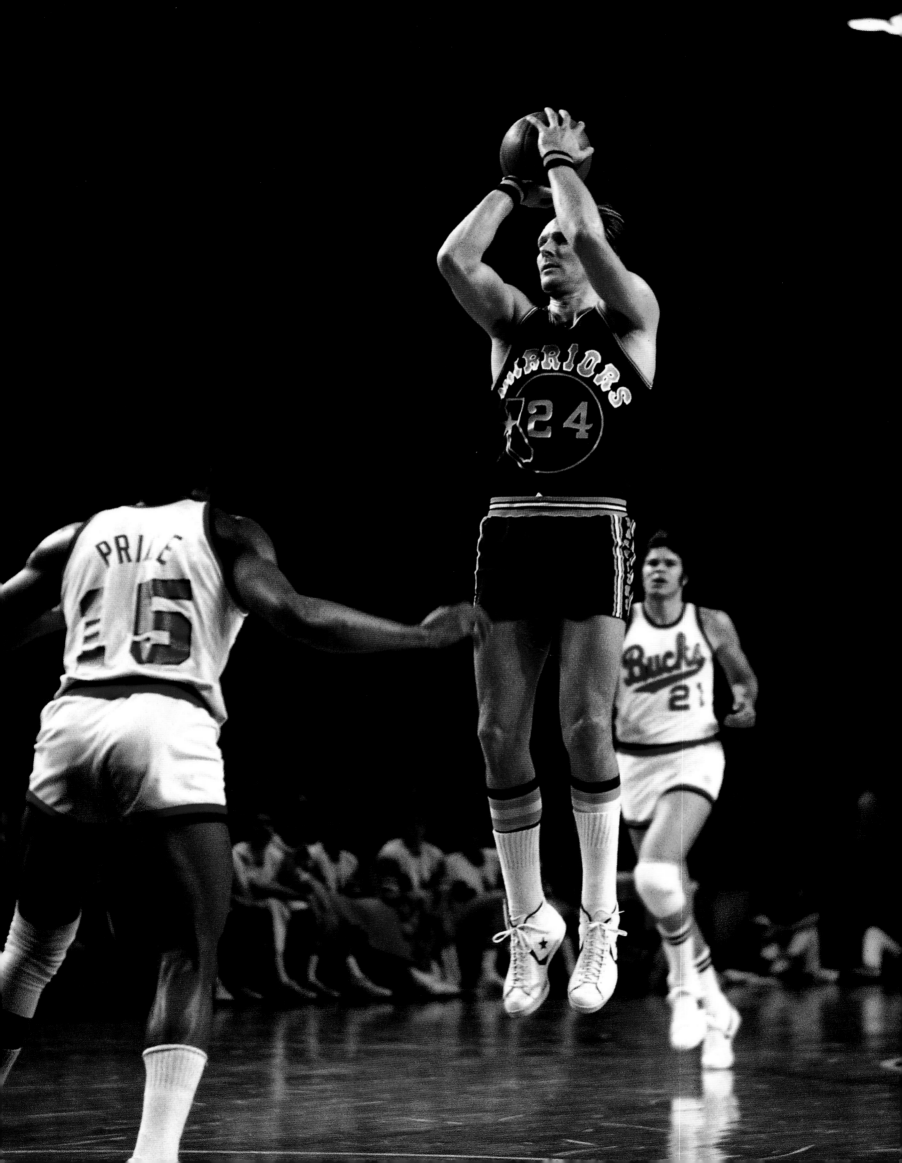

Rick Barry's signature move? Putting the ball in the hoop. And he wasn't picky about how he did it.

The 6-foot-7 Barry was one of the greatest pure scorers ever. His arsenal of scoring moves — headlined by a textbook jump shot — included dribble drives, fadeaways, pull-ups, running one-handers and so on. He made 90 percent of his free-throw attempts utilizing an unorthodox underhand method.

A coach's son, Barry strove for perfection from an early age. His single-minded determination made him a great player but also helped make him a polarizing figure. Combative and demanding of himself and of others, Barry incurred the wrath of opponents, fans, referees and even teammates.

"I was never the most popular player because I never went out to make friends," Barry said after he retired. "I went out to win games."

In the process, Barry posted some jaw-dropping numbers. At the University of Miami, he averaged 32.2 points as a junior and an NCAA-high 37.4 points per game as a senior. He played 14 pro seasons (10 in the NBA and four in the American Basketball Association), winning a championship in each league while tallying 25,279 points and averaging 24.8 points per game. Barry scored 363 points in 10 NBA Finals games for a record average of 36.3, and he is the only player ever to lead the NCAA, NBA and ABA in scoring.

In the 1975 NBA Finals, Barry led the Golden State Warriors to a stunning sweep of the heavily favored Washington Bullets. Barry averaged 29.5 points, 5.0 assists and 3.5 steals per game during the series to garner the NBA Finals MVP Award.

"It has to be the greatest upset in the history of the NBA Finals," Barry said. "It was like a fairy-tale season….It's something I'll treasure for the rest of my life."

When Elgin Baylor arrived, the NBA was cleared for takeoff.

The aerial acrobatics that bring NBA fans to their feet began with the 6-foot-5 forward, who played 14 seasons for the Lakers. His legatees — including Connie Hawkins, Julius Erving and Michael Jordan — are better known, but Baylor was the first high-flyer.

"I never tried to be like anybody," Baylor said. "I just played the game my way."

The high-jumping Baylor was a complete player who could handle the ball, knock down perimeter shots, post up, play defense and crash the boards — his career average of 13.5 rebounds per game ranks ninth in NBA history. He was too tall and strong for backcourt players, and his quickness and athleticism left big men clutching at air.

He displayed amazing creativity, especially around the rim. Baylor had "hang time" before the term was coined. Suspended in midair, he could change his direction or his shot, frustrating defenders and leaving observers awestruck.

"He never broke the law of gravity, but he's awfully slow about obeying it," a columnist wrote of Baylor.

In 1957-58, the Minneapolis Lakers went 19-53 and nearly folded. Enter Baylor, who led the Lakers to the 1959 NBA Finals as a rookie. The next year, the franchise moved from Minneapolis to Los Angeles and Baylor teamed with Jerry West to form one of the greatest tandems in NBA history. The duo led the Lakers to seven NBA Finals in nine years, though they never won. The 1971-72 Lakers finally won a championship, but without Baylor, who had retired nine games into the season.

During his first five seasons, Baylor was the NBA's most dominant player not named Wilt Chamberlain, averaging 32 points per game. Though later slowed by injuries, his career average of 27.4 points per game still ranks fourth in NBA history.

In the 1966 NBA Draft, the Detroit Pistons and their fans had their sights set on Cazzie Russell, a star guard who played nearby at the University of Michigan. But their hopes were dashed when they lost a coin flip to the New York Knicks.

Detroit's "consolation prize" turned out to be one of the greatest players in franchise history and a future mayor of the city.

Dave Bing, a 6-foot-3 guard, had put Syracuse's basketball program on the map, leading the school in scoring in all three of his varsity seasons. He did all that despite impaired vision in his left eye, the result of a childhood injury. In Detroit, he stepped into the starting lineup and quickly won over the Pistons' fans with his humble attitude and graceful style. Bing had a smooth jump shot and a terrific floor sense, delivering passes that surprised opponents and sometimes even the intended recipient.

Bing scored 20.0 points per game in 1966-67 to win the NBA Rookie of the Year Award. He only got better from there, averaging 20 or more points per game in each of his first seven seasons, including a career-high 27.1 points per game in 1967-68, when he led the NBA with 2,142 points. His teammates elected him captain, and in 1973-74, he led the Pistons to 52 victories, a franchise record (since broken).

Bing played nine seasons in Detroit, averaging 22.6 points per game. He finished his career by playing two seasons in Washington and one in Boston until recurring vision problems (he had injured his right eye as well, in 1970) forced him to retire. He returned to Detroit, where he had worked in the steel industry each offseason, and started a steel service company. A decade later the firm was grossing more than $60 million a year. In 2009, Bing was elected mayor of Detroit.

Larry Bird's first pro coach said that Bird couldn't outrun Boston Celtics President Red Auerbach, who was 63 years old at the time. Bird joked that his vertical leap was "three or four inches."

Such claims were exaggeration — Bird actually possessed considerable athletic ability — but they made for a good story. No doubt it also helped spur him on during the thousands of hours he spent practicing, first in his driveway and later in the gym. Others may have run faster or jumped higher, but none worked harder than Larry Joe Bird.

That work ethic helped make the 6-foot-9 forward one of the greatest players ever. He shot with picture-perfect form, excelled as a rebounder and played solid defense. His skill as a passer thwarted double teams, and there were none better in the clutch.

Bird's greatest asset might have been his court sense. Like a chess champion, he saw several moves ahead.

"Everyone in the country knows he can shoot. Other things impress me more," Auerbach said after the Celtics drafted Bird. "He has a great concept of the game, a great feel of what's going on between the four lines."

Bird played 13 seasons for the Celtics, from 1979 to 1992. He led Boston to three titles, and he is one of only three players to win three consecutive NBA MVP Awards. After retiring as a player, Bird went on to become the first person to win the MVP, Coach of the Year (with the Indiana Pacers in 1997-98) and Executive of the Year Awards (Pacers, 2011-12).

"Larry was the only player in the league that I feared, and the smartest player I ever played against," said former Lakers great Magic Johnson when Bird retired. The Bird-Magic rivalry defined the game during the 1980s and helped revitalize the NBA.

At his first press conference as a Los Angeles Laker, 17-year-old Kobe Bryant made a promise.

"I know they're going to try to go at me. It's all part of the challenge of playing in the NBA," Bryant said in 1996. "I'm young, but I'm not going to back down from anyone."

True to his word, Bryant has never backed down from any challenge, and that competitive fire has helped make him one of the greatest players in NBA history. The teenager has become a grizzled veteran, but he remains indomitable.

"Father Time will eventually catch up," Bryant, then 33, said in February 2012. "It's not going to catch up this year. Maybe it will be next year. Maybe it will be the year after that. That's the kind of challenge that I enjoy going through."

Bryant showed no signs of slowing down in his 16th NBA season, as he nearly won the 2011-12 NBA scoring crown with 27.9 points per game. He finished the season ranked fifth on the NBA's all-time list with 29,484 points, which he amassed utilizing an unparalleled array of moves. The 6-foot-6 Bryant, arguably the most versatile and complete offensive player ever, adds a new move or two every offseason, all in pursuit of one goal.

"Kobe's drive, since I met him when he was 16, is to be the best player in the world," said former teammate Lamar Odom. "He wants to go down as one of the best players — if not *the* best player — to ever play the game."

For Bryant, being the best means winning championships. He has five NBA titles, but he wants more.

"I'm obsessed about it," Bryant said. "I watched (Larry) Bird, I watched Magic (Johnson)…I watched (Michael) Jordan win multiple titles. I just kind of grew up saying, 'This is how it should be. This is what I must do.'"

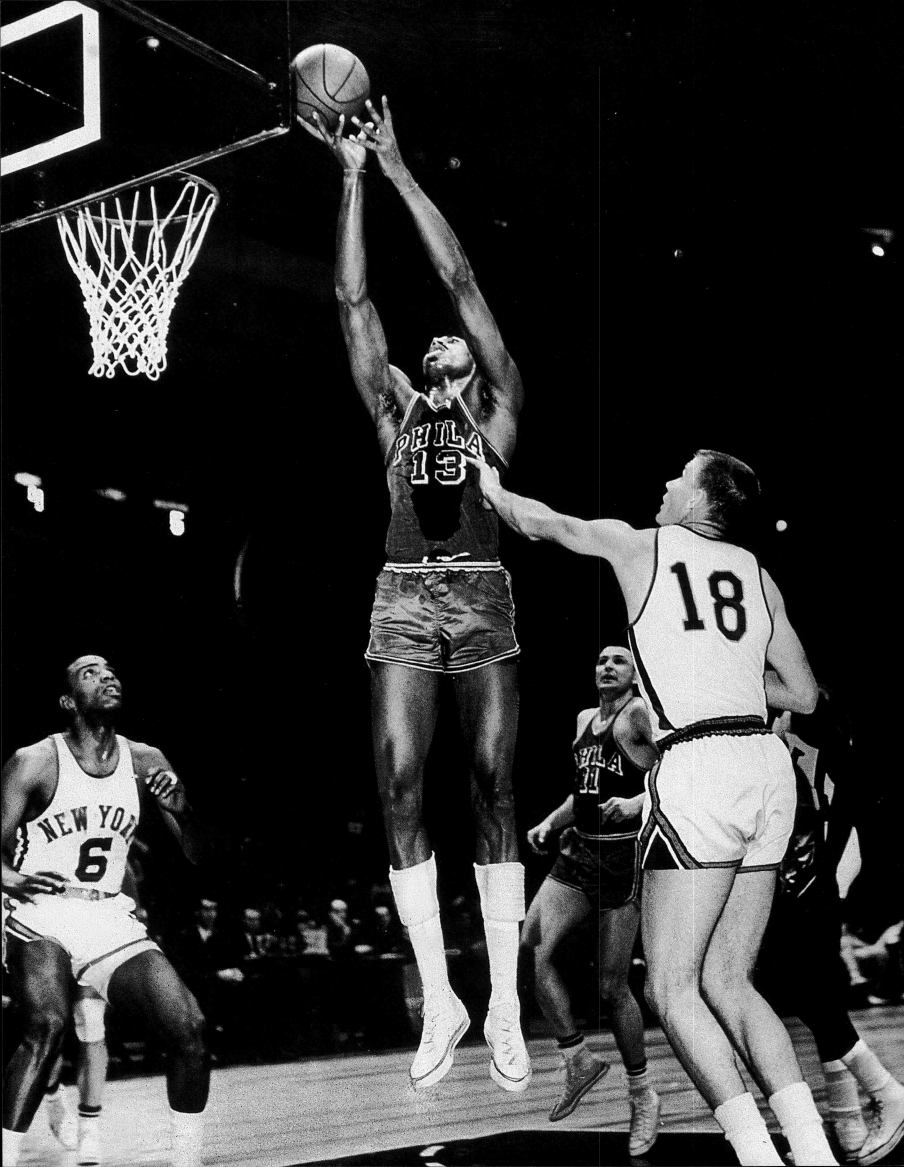

There is domination, and then there is what Wilt Chamberlain did during his 14 seasons in the NBA.

A sampling: Seven scoring titles, 11 rebounding titles, eight years leading the league in minutes, nine years leading the league in field-goal percentage. One season he led the NBA in total assists, the only non-guard to accomplish that feat.

Sure, Chamberlain had the size — he stood 7-foot-1 and weighed 275 pounds — but he also was a fantastic athlete. His strength was legendary, as was his conditioning (he averaged nearly 46 minutes per game during his NBA career).

Chamberlain, already famous from his college days at Kansas, joined the Philadelphia Warriors in 1959, and averaged 37.6 points and 27.0 rebounds per game to become the first man to win the NBA Rookie of the Year and NBA MVP Awards in the same season. But Wilt was just warming up. In 1961-62, he averaged 50.4 points per game, including a 100-point effort against the New York Knicks. Both marks are NBA records that have never been threatened and likely never will be.

Always a rebounding monster (he is the NBA's all-time leader), later in his career Chamberlain became less of a scorer and more of a passer and defender. He owns the four highest single-season scoring averages in NBA history. The "Big Dipper" won two NBA titles, with the Philadelphia 76ers in 1967 and the Los Angeles Lakers in 1972, and finished with four NBA MVP Awards. He still owns or shares 72 NBA records.

"Nobody seems to appreciate what an incredible player Wilt was," legendary Celtics center Bill Russell said in 1996 when the two were named to the NBA's 50th Anniversary Team. "He was the best player of all time because he dominated the floor like nobody else ever could. To be that big and that athletic was special."

Bob Cousy performed magic with the basketball, earning him the moniker "Houdini of the Hardwood." His popularity transcended the sport, netting him endorsement deals and the NBA's first *Sports Illustrated* cover ("Bob Cousy: Basketball's Genius"). Kids tried to duplicate his moves on playgrounds across America.

"The Celtics wouldn't be here without him," said Walter Brown, the Boston franchise's owner and founder, upon Cousy's retirement in 1963. "If he had played in New York, I think he would have been as big as Babe Ruth. I think he is anyway."

The NBA's first superstar may not have played in New York but he learned the game there. Cousy traded stickball for basketball at age 12 when he and his French immigrant parents moved from a Manhattan tenement to a house in Queens. Skilled hoops players abounded in Cousy's new neighborhood, stirring his competitive streak and inspiring him to greatness.

Today everybody plays like "The Cooz," or at least tries to, but he was the first — the first point guard, the first magic man, the first human highlight film. He relentlessly pushed the ball on offense, attacking the rim to score or more often to dish to a teammate. He could alter his pass or shot in midair, and easily shed full-court pressure with behind-the-back dribbles. He surprised defenders (and sometimes teammates) with no-look passes, thanks to his remarkable peripheral vision. The 6-foot-1 Cousy played taller thanks to large hands and long arms.

After a record-setting career at Holy Cross, Cousy played 13 seasons (1950-1963) for Boston, leading the signature fast break that propelled the Celtics' dynasty. "The Cooz" garnered All-NBA First Team honors 10 times, topped the NBA in assists eight consecutive seasons, won the 1956-57 NBA MVP Award, and led the Celtics to six championships in a seven-year span from 1957 to 1963.

During the 1950s and '60s, Red Auerbach built the Boston Celtics' dynasty around 6-foot-9 Bill Russell, a unique center who used his intelligence and athleticism to dominate the middle. After Russell retired, Auerbach found another undersized gem — Dave Cowens — to spark Boston's rebirth.

Many doubted whether Cowens, at 6-foot-9 and 230 pounds, could play center in the NBA. The doubters included Auerbach, who had retired from coaching in 1966 but still served as the Celtics' general manager. He tried to move his prized rookie to forward, but Cowens balked, and after a talk with Russell, Auerbach left him at center.

Cowens played the position like no one had before. He seemed to be in perpetual motion, especially on offense. He outhustled everyone, leaving guards and big men alike staggering in his wake. He dominated the glass with his aggressiveness, while his leaping ability, quickness and long arms more than compensated for his lack of bulk.

"He's so quick he's like a 6-9 Jerry West," said New York Knicks center Jerry Lucas, comparing Cowens to the legendary Los Angeles Lakers guard who was also known for his intensity. "One minute he's standing in front of you and the next he's gone, rolling toward the basket or straight up in the air shooting his jumper. It's like he disappears."

Cowens played 10 seasons in Boston (1970-1980) and one in Milwaukee (1982-83). He led the Celtics to NBA titles in 1974 and 1976, and won the 1972-73 NBA MVP Award. He averaged 14 rebounds per game during his Celtics career, and assuredly was never outworked.

"I never thought of myself as a superstar," Cowens said in 1991, when he was inducted into the Naismith Memorial Basketball Hall of Fame. "I represent the working class of the NBA. I'm honored they selected me because I could name a whole lot of guys who were better than Dave Cowens."

BILLYCUNNINGHAM

For his fifth birthday, Billy Cunningham received a basketball. It was love at first sight.

Cunningham took the ball to the local court and has never been far from the game since, achieving great success at every level. He became a New York City high school basketball legend and then headed to the University of North Carolina. Dean Smith, who had just become the Tar Heels' coach, recalled later that he looked at the skinny new recruit and thought, "How in the world can this kid play ball? He can't even walk."

Not only could 6-foot-7 Cunningham walk, he could jump, and he was hyper-competitive. His amazing leaping ability earned him the nickname "the Kangaroo Kid" and he became one of the greatest players in North Carolina's storied history, averaging 24.8 points and 15.4 rebounds per game in his collegiate career.

Cunningham went on to play 11 pro seasons, nine with the Philadelphia 76ers (1965-1972, 1974-76) and two with the ABA's Carolina Cougars (1972-74). He was an electric presence on the court, fearless and intense with a deadly left-handed jumper. He was the sixth man for the 1966-67 Sixers team that many consider the greatest in NBA history. That season, Philadelphia went 68-13 and ended the Boston Celtics' eight-year run as NBA champions. Cunningham led the Sixers in scoring four consecutive seasons and then jumped leagues, winning the 1972-73 ABA MVP Award.

After a knee injury forced Cunningham to retire at age 32, he coached the 76ers for eight seasons (1977-1985). He guided Philadelphia to three appearances in the NBA Finals, including a sweep of the Los Angeles Lakers in 1983. He finished with a regular-season record of 454-196, and his winning percentage (.698) is second only to Phil Jackson (.704) in NBA history.

From 1987 to 1995, Cunningham was part owner of the Miami Heat.

Adrian Dantley faced doubters his entire life — too fat, too short, too slow, they said. They were all wrong. The numbers don't lie.

"In a way, the labels were good," Dantley said in 1988. "I wasn't supposed to be an all-pro, an all-star, so I worked harder."

Working harder meant never taking a day off, even Christmas. Working harder meant jumping rope all summer and spending hours on end in the gym, often alone. There he honed his smooth jump shot and developed the terrific footwork, head fakes, pump fakes and spin moves that allowed him to score over anyone, no matter how tall. Though only 6-foot-5, he lived in the paint and on the free-throw line.

Dantley had to overcome skeptics at each stop. At DeMatha High School in Maryland, his doughy physique earned him the nickname "Baby Huey." Whatever they called him, Dantley led DeMatha to a 57-2 record. Supposedly too short to play forward in college, Dantley averaged 25.8 points per game in three seasons at Notre Dame, then led the U.S. team to the gold medal at the 1976 Olympics.

"Adrian Dantley was an absolute dominant college basketball player," former Notre Dame coach Digger Phelps said in 2008, when Dantley was inducted into the Naismith Memorial Basketball Hall of Fame. "He was more than capable of taking over games by himself, and he was an absolute fierce competitor."

Dantley played 15 seasons in the NBA — including seven in Utah and three in Detroit — from 1976 to 1991. His career average of 24.3 points per game ranks 16th in league history through the 2011-12 season, and he ranks 21st in career field-goal percentage (.540), making him the shortest player among the NBA's top 25 in that category. He twice led the NBA in scoring, and his total of 23,177 points still ranks 22nd in 2012.

Dave DeBusschere played 12 seasons in the NBA. He played professional baseball as a pitcher. He is the only man in basketball history to be a player, coach, general manager and league commissioner (he led the ABA during the 1970s). But he is best remembered as "the final piece of the puzzle."

The New York Knicks were 18-17 when they sent their starting center and a starting guard to Detroit for DeBusschere on Dec. 19, 1968. Everything fell into place for the Knicks after that. The 6-foot-6 power forward shined as a defensive stopper and rebounder with some streaky shooting bursts. Willis Reed moved from forward to center, his natural position, Bill Bradley moved from guard to small forward, and Walt Frazier became the starting point guard.

That lineup went 36-11 the rest of the 1968-69 season and gave the Celtics a scare before losing in the 1969 Eastern Division Finals. The Knicks then advanced to three NBA Finals in the next four seasons, winning it all in 1970 and 1973.

"We made some great trades, but this one has to be considered the best," said Knicks coach Red Holzman. "That made us a great team."

Emphasis was on the word "team." Individually, the Knicks' players were good; together, they were great. They executed Holzman's vision — "find the open man" and "play defense as a team" — by making the extra pass and trusting their teammates. Without a doubt, DeBusschere was the Knicks' heart and soul, "the glue" as one teammate described him. He often played hurt but never at anything less than full-tilt.

"Dave's strength, his dedication, his unselfishness, his fierce desire to win, and above all, his commitment to the team, were all at the core of his success," Bradley said during his eulogy for DeBusschere, who died in 2003. "He seemed to say, 'What's the point of achieving anything in basketball if you can't share it?'"

C lyde Drexler entered the NBA without much of a jump shot. He hadn't needed it at the University of Houston, where he headed the "fraternity" known as "Phi Slamma Jamma." Drexler and his Cougar teammates excelled at more high-percentage shots, usually taken from above the rim.

"Clyde was a great college player whose feet rarely touched the ground," said Portland Trail Blazers scout Bucky Buckwalter.

Portland selected Drexler with the 14th pick in the 1983 NBA Draft, and he quickly discovered that speed and leaping ability were not enough. Many NBA players were fast and could jump. Under the tutelage of Blazers coach Jack Ramsay, "Clyde the Glide" developed into a complete player, and one of the game's best all-around players for the next decade.

Drexler alternated among three positions — both guard spots and small forward — and filled up the stat sheet every night with points, rebounds, assists and steals. His dunks, some of which began with him taking flight from the free-throw line, are the stuff of legend. He averaged 21.5 or more points per game in six consecutive seasons, from 1986-87 through 1991-92, and propelled the high-octane offense of the "Rip City" Blazers to two NBA Finals appearances. He also won a gold medal as part of the "Dream Team" at the 1992 Olympics.

Late in his career Drexler became more of a ball-handler, passer and 3-point shooter, although he still showed flashes of "Clyde the Glide." He returned to his hometown of Houston in a 1995 trade and helped the Rockets win the NBA title that year.

When Drexler retired in 1998, he was the only NBA player in history to have amassed at least 20,000 points, 6,000 rebounds, 6,000 assists and 2,000 steals. He is Portland's career leader in points, rebounds and minutes.

Shaquille O'Neal nicknamed him "The Big Fundamental" because his game is so technically perfect. San Antonio Spurs coach Gregg Popovich said "he may be a 7-footer, but he is basically a quarterback in shorts." Numerous others have called him the best power forward ever, a superb scorer, passer, rebounder and defender.

Everyone sings Tim Duncan's praises. Everyone, that is, except Tim Duncan.

"He's basically an introverted, quite humorous, highly intelligent, easygoing guy who has gotten over himself," said Popovich.

"No, he doesn't care about being the best player in the world," said former teammate Robert Horry. "He only cares about winning."

Duncan has done plenty of winning since he arrived in San Antonio in 1997, leading the Spurs to 15 consecutive playoff appearances — the longest active streak in the NBA through 2011-12 — and four NBA titles. The Spurs ask a lot of Duncan at both ends of the floor, but nothing he can't handle.

"He's one person who impacts every single aspect of the game," former teammate David Robinson told *USA Today* in 2007. "Everything you ask him to do he is able to do."

Duncan is the most complete post-up player in the game, with exquisite footwork and a variety of moves. Nobody has used the glass more than Duncan, who can bank it in from anywhere, often at an angle that seems to defy geometry. He excels at almost every facet of the game except self-promotion, though that has not stopped Duncan from earning nine All-NBA First Team selections, two NBA MVP Awards and three NBA Finals MVP Awards.

"He is getting older, just like you are, and all of us, but Tim Duncan is still the backbone of our program," Popovich said of his 36-year-old star during the 2012 NBA Playoffs. "He's the guy we build around. He sets the tone for us."

KEVIN DURANT

After his first five NBA seasons, from 2007 to 2012, Kevin Durant had three consecutive scoring titles, nearly 10,000 points, a trip to the NBA Finals and a career average of 26.3 points per game — all before he celebrated his 24th birthday.

No wonder they call Durant "the player with no ceiling." Prodigious talent and a dedicated work ethic have helped make the Oklahoma City forward one of the best players in the game, not that he would ever make such a claim. But his desire to be great burns so brightly that others have taken note.

"A 6-foot-11 me," said Lakers guard Kobe Bryant, one of the game's most driven players, comparing Durant to himself.

He's not quite that height, although the 6-foot-9 Durant has such long arms that he seems taller. Always tall, he loved basketball from an early age. The desire to be great was apparent even then, which his why Taras Brown, his youth coach and godfather, made him repeatedly write "Hard Work Beats Talent When Talent Fails to Work" before a tournament.

Durant got the message. He earned a scholarship to Texas, where he averaged 25.8 points and 11.1 rebounds per game as a freshman. Despite questions about his durability, he was the second player chosen in the 2007 NBA Draft. Nobody asks about his durability any more. Now, the only question is how high can he fly? Durant, for one, plans to keep chasing perfection, even if unattainable.

"There's always another level you can go to. In basketball, you can always be better at something," Durant said during the 2012 NBA Finals. "I haven't seen a guy that totally dominates the game in every aspect. He can't make every shot, he can't get every rebound, [and] he can't get every assist, so I think you can get better. That's the mindset I take."

ALEX ENGLISH

Which NBA player scored the most points during the 1980s? Larry Bird? Magic Johnson? Julius Erving? Michael Jordan? Try Alex English.

No matter how high he soared, the 6-foot-7 English somehow stayed under the radar.

"I'm low-key. My job is to do the job I'm supposed to do," English said. "There are people who don't see it, but they're not paying attention."

The NBA did not pay attention, at least initially. After starring at the University of South Carolina, English languished on the Milwaukee Bucks' bench for two seasons. He signed with Indiana as a free agent, and just as he began to flourish, the Pacers traded him to the Denver Nuggets on Feb. 1, 1980.

"Going to Denver was probably the best thing that ever happened to me," English said.

Indeed. During his decade in Denver, the graceful and elegant forward set an NBA record (since broken) by scoring 2,000 or more points in eight consecutive seasons. English won the 1982-83 scoring crown (28.4 points per game) and led the Nuggets to nine straight playoff appearances.

Though he weighed just 190 pounds, English displayed amazing durability (he played 80 or more games in 12 different seasons). He finished his 15-year career — he also played one season in Dallas — with 25,613 points, which still ranked 13th on the all-time list through the 2011-12 season.

"It wasn't about the money for me, it was more about my art, which was my game — my ability to play and how I played and what I could do on the basketball court," English said.

He created art off the court as well, publishing several books of poetry. English, who received the 1988 J. Walter Kennedy Citizenship Award from the NBA for his community service efforts, is a regular participant in the NBA's Basketball Without Borders program. He returned to the NBA in 2003 as an assistant coach.

JULIUS ERVING

Before the kids wanted to "be like Mike," as in Michael Jordan, they wanted to be Dr. J. No player has had as great an impact on the NBA as Julius Erving. Who says? Magic Johnson, that's who.

"Julius Erving did more to popularize basketball than anybody else who's ever played the game," said Johnson. "There were other big players, talented players before him, but it was Dr. J who put the 'Wow!' into the game."

Erving began putting the "Wow!" in the game when he turned pro in 1971. He went from college hoops, where dunking was outlawed, to the American Basketball Association, basketball's version of the Wild West. The Doctor, freed from any limits, made moves that no one had ever seen before, and in some cases, since.

Erving didn't jump so much as levitate, the ball clutched in his huge hand as if it were an extension of his arm. He seemed to defy gravity as he stayed aloft, often twisting or spinning in midair to evade a defender. He could finish with a dunk, or lay in a finger-roll — with either hand. Erving compared it to making jazz, each riff a little different than the last.

He possessed a complete game — shooting, defense, rebounding, passing — but the artistry he displayed on a nightly basis made him a transcendent star. Dr. J put fans in the seats and then brought them out of those seats.

"I had my own style," Erving said. "Call it playground, call it street ball or whatever. It was about pushing the limits, testing my own imagination."

Erving, the only player to win a championship and the MVP Award in both the ABA and NBA, scored 30,026 points in 16 pro seasons to rank fifth on the combined ABA/NBA all-time list through the 2011-12 season. Those numbers only hint at the Doctor's legacy, which actually can be seen everyday on basketball courts worldwide.

On March 1, 2003, No. 33 was hoisted from the rafters at Madison Square Garden, never to be worn again by another New York Knicks player.

"You just don't know the joy I feel inside," said Patrick Ewing. "I would like to thank all you fans. We had our ups and downs… but I think for the most part, you all definitely showed me that you appreciated everything I did."

All No. 33 did was revive a moribund franchise. When Ewing showed up in 1985, the Knicks had been wandering in the basketball wilderness for more than a decade. The 7-foot center from Georgetown led them back into the limelight. He was a terrific defender, determined to challenge any shot he could. Though unpolished offensively, he developed into a solid low-post scorer. He spent 15 of his 17 NBA seasons in New York, leading the Knicks to 13 playoff berths and averaging 22.8 points and 10.4 rebounds per game.

Though Ewing's résumé lacks an NBA title, it's not for lack of trying. He was a "true warrior," in the words of Pat Riley, his former coach. Riley's grueling workouts scared off many a player, but his superstar center relished the marathon sessions and asked for more. An immigrant who didn't touch a basketball until he was age 12, Ewing never took his NBA stardom for granted.

"I tell my father that every time he and I go visit my mother's grave, I sit there and I tell her thank you for bringing me to this country because back in Jamaica, who knows what I would be," Ewing said in 2003. "But they brought me here to America, and I learned this game of basketball, and it brought me everything I could imagine — fame, fortune, respect from my peers. And that means a lot."

WALTFRAZIER

Walt Frazier is synonymous with New York. He played 10 of his 13 NBA seasons for the Knicks, and since 1987 he has been the voice of the team on its television broadcasts. But his New York story goes back even further than that.

In 1967, Frazier garnered MVP honors while leading Southern Illinois to the National Invitational Tournament title at Madison Square Garden. The New York crowds loved him, and Frazier found the city captivating. But it seemed unlikely that an unheralded guard like himself could play for the Knicks.

The Knicks, however, had scouted him in the NIT, and they selected him fifth overall in the 1967 NBA Draft. He took over as the starting point guard in his second season, and led New York to NBA titles in 1970 and 1973. In Game 7 of the 1970 NBA Finals, Frazier put together one of the greatest performances in NBA postseason history with 36 points and 19 assists.

Though Frazier was inconsistent on offense, he found a way to score in big games and in fourth quarters, or he found the teammate with the hot hand. His defense, however, was consistently spectacular.

"I like to keep them guessing where I am," Frazier said. "I have the advantage because my hands are so quick. It's like I'm playing possum — I'm there but I don't look like I'm there."

After the final buzzer, he slipped into his "Clyde" persona, so named from the movie "Bonnie and Clyde" because of Frazier's penchant for fancy suits and fedoras. He was stylish and ahead of his time.

"A lot of guys today credit me as the first guy with the bling," Frazier said in 2009. "That was part of the fun of being in New York then. We were winning, and we had the hoopla back in the 1970s."

Some players put on their "game face" to get ready for tipoff. Kevin Garnett never takes his off.

"I don't know if he's never not [intense]," said Boston Celtics coach Doc Rivers. "I never had a player like him."

Nor has any other coach. KG's motor is always running at full throttle, whether he is alone in the gym during the summer or playing in Game 7 of the NBA Finals.

"I've learned not to fight it, to just let it sort of ooze its way out and play," Garnett said in 2008. "To let the adrenaline flow, let it run."

He entered the NBA as "Da Kid," immensely talented but so young. The Minnesota Timberwolves took a chance by selecting the 18-year-old Garnett, and he repaid them by becoming their franchise player. KG was a unique 6-foot-11 forward who played facing the basket, knocked down outside shots and ran the floor on fast breaks. He covered the entire floor on defense, battling big men in the middle, switching on picks to cover guards, and coming across the lane to block shots. He never seemed to tire, and he hardly missed a game.

After 12 seasons (1995-2007) in Minnesota, Garnett joined the Celtics, where his defensive mindset and unselfish play on offense meshed perfectly into Rivers' system. KG received much of the credit for Boston's 42-game improvement in 2007-08, as the Celtics finished with the NBA's best record at 66-16.

"Everything he's done for the culture of the team, his impact on the game, is just tremendous," Celtics guard Paul Pierce said.

Garnett helped the Celtics win the 2008 NBA title — the franchise's first championship in 22 years — and narrowly missed winning again in 2010. Garnett is equally tireless off the court, and his many efforts to aid the community earned him the 2006 J. Walter Kennedy Citizenship Award from the NBA.

As a shy teenager growing up in difficult circumstances, George Gervin went into the gym almost every night and shut out the world. The school custodian let Gervin play one-on-none every night, so long as he swept the floor.

"It gave me solitude," Gervin said. "I was alone in there for hours. There was nothing but me and my imagination."

Those solo sessions produced one of the greatest offensive players in basketball history. The 6-foot-7 Gervin scored every way imaginable, from long-range jumpers to runners in the lane, from turnaround shots to acrobatic layups. He exhibited amazing body control and had an answer for every kind of defense. "The Iceman" was so smooth he made it look easy.

"You don't stop George Gervin," said Washington Bullets coach Dick Motta. "You just hope that his arm gets tired after 40 shots. I believe the guy can score whenever he wants to. I wonder if he gets bored out there."

Gervin played 14 pro seasons — four in the ABA (1972-76) and a decade (1976-1986) in the NBA. His total of 26,595 points ranked 14th on the all-time ABA/NBA list through 2012, and his four NBA scoring titles are surpassed only by Michael Jordan and Wilt Chamberlain. San Antonio, where Gervin played 11 1/2 seasons, retired his No. 44 in 1987.

One of those scoring crowns came in 1977-78, when Gervin dropped 63 points on the New Orleans Jazz — including an NBA-record 33 in the second quarter — in the season finale to finish at 27.22 points per game and edge out Denver's David Thompson (27.15).

"Nobody else could have done it," said Spurs coach Doug Moe. "New Orleans put three guys on him and didn't even guard a couple of our guys, and he still scored. He put on one of the most amazing shows I have ever seen."

Hal Greer starred at Douglass High School in his hometown of Huntington, West Virginia. He earned a scholarship to nearby Marshall — the first African-American to do so — and starred there as well, averaging 19.4 points per game. Yet when Greer showed up for his first NBA training camp with the Syracuse Nationals, he all but told the taxi driver to wait.

"I didn't think I had a chance at all," Greer recalled later. "In fact, when I first got there I didn't even unpack my bag."

As it turned out, Greer stayed a while — 15 seasons, to be exact, first in Syracuse, and later in Philadelphia, where the club moved and became the 76ers. He was the franchise's cornerstone from 1958 to 1973.

"Hal Greer always came to play," said former teammate and coach Dolph Schayes in 1982, when Greer was inducted into the Hall of Fame. "He came to practice the same way. Every bus and plane and train, he was on time. Hal Greer punched the clock. Hal Greer brought the lunch pail."

The 6-foot-2 Greer was a marvel of consistency, averaging 18 points or more per game in 11 consecutive seasons. He had a fluid pull-up jumper that he launched from the top of the key, maybe the most dependable midrange shot in NBA history. He even used that jump shot on his free throws, which he made at an 80 percent clip.

"Hal Greer was such a smart player," said Sixers teammate Billy Cunningham. "In his mind he had a book about every player he played against and what he had to do to make sure he got free to get shots."

Greer is still the Sixers' all-time leader in a number of categories, including points (21,586). He averaged 27.7 points per game during the 1967 playoffs to lead Philadelphia to the NBA title.

The Boston Celtics, coming off their fourth consecutive NBA title, selected John Havlicek in the 1962 NBA Draft with the modest hope that he would replace Frank Ramsey as the team's sixth man.

Havlicek turned out to be so much more than that. One of the game's greatest all-around players, his arrival allowed Boston to extend its dynasty past its logical expiration date. "Hondo" was a bridge between eras — his first season was Bob Cousy's last, and he retired one year before Larry Bird arrived — and the embodiment of Celtic pride.

A terrific athlete who had also been drafted by the National Football League, the 6-foot-5 swingman overpowered guards, yet his quickness left frontcourt players flat-footed. He worked relentlessly to develop into a complete player, and he played with intensity from tipoff until the final buzzer. The Celtics' sixth man helped Boston win six titles during the 1960s.

"One thing I learned from Red Auerbach was that it's not who starts the game, but who finishes it, and I generally was around at the finish," Havlicek said.

After Bill Russell retired in 1969, Havlicek went from being the best non-starter in the league to simply being the best, filling up the stat sheet while playing 45 minutes per game. He led the Celtics to titles in 1974 and 1976, giving him eight championships, and he retired in 1978 as the franchise's all-time leading scorer.

"On stamina alone he'd be among the top players who ever played the game," said New York Knicks coach Red Holzman. "It would've been fair to those who had to play him or those who had to coach against him if he had been blessed only with his inhuman endurance. God had to compound it by making him a good scorer, smart ball-handler and intelligent defensive player with quickness of mind, hands and feet."

ELVIN HAYES

Elvin Hayes first picked up a basketball in the eighth grade, but he was so clumsy that his feeble efforts elicited only laughter. By ninth grade he was no longer an object of ridicule, though he still wasn't good enough to make the freshman team.

"I was too weak to shoot the turnaround then," Hayes recalled later, "so all summer long I shot with a small rubber ball at a basket in my yard."

That summer and every summer in high school, Hayes practiced 11 hours a day (by his estimation). He worked on his turnaround jumper and other moves he would need to score over Boston Celtics center Bill Russell, who was his favorite player. Those imaginary battles with Russell proved to be his ticket to a college scholarship and, as it turned out, NBA stardom.

Hayes grew to 6-foot-9 and became a dominating power forward at the University of Houston. In 1968, in one of the greatest college basketball games ever, Hayes tallied 39 points and 15 rebounds to lead the Cougars to a 71-69 win over UCLA. More than 50,000 fans in the Astrodome and millions more on television watched Houston end UCLA's 47-game winning streak. The legend of the "Big E" was born.

Hayes went on to play 16 seasons (1968-1984) in the NBA, mostly at power forward but also at center. He missed just nine games in his career, a remarkable achievement considering the physical battles he faced every game. Though undersized for a center, his power and turnaround jumper allowed him to succeed against much taller players.

Hayes played the majority of his career (nine seasons) with the Bullets, helping Washington win the 1978 NBA title. Hayes' total of 27,313 points still ranked eighth in 2012, and his 50,000 career minutes ranked third.

At the 2008 NBA Slam Dunk contest, Dwight Howard pulled off his Orlando Magic jersey to reveal a Superman shirt. He completed the outfit by donning a red cape, and then raced toward the hoop, catching a pass in midair and slamming it home.

"This one was really for the big men," Howard said after becoming the first center to win the contest, garnering 78 percent of the fan vote. "People say big men don't look good dunking. I really wanted to win it for all the big men."

The 6-foot-11 Howard is the biggest of the NBA's big men today, not in height but rather in stature. He also is one of the few "traditional" centers in today's NBA, a post-up player who sets up with his back to the basket. He is a defensive terror who so controls the middle that opponents have to alter their offensive strategy. Howard not only shuts down his man, but he helps out teammates and owns the glass.

Early in his career, his offensive game consisted of putbacks of missed shots and dunks after an opponent's mistake on defense. His repertoire has expanded since, and Howard has averaged 20 or more points per game since 2007. Plus he looks good dunking and can run the floor on the break.

He earned his fifth consecutive All-NBA First Team selection in 2011-12, adding to a collection of honors that already includes three NBA Defensive Player of the Year Awards. Howard proudly admits that he does not fit the usual image of an intimidating big man with a menacing glare.

"Basketball brings me joy and I'm having fun blocking shots and dunking, so I am going to smile," Howard wrote on his blog. "I'm going to smile and have fun, but at the same time I'm still going to dunk on you."

Longtime NBA coach Pat Riley nicknamed Allen Iverson "Pound for Pound," as in "pound for pound the toughest player in the game."

His toughness and passion were never questioned. His judgement, however, is another matter. Any time the smallest player on the floor keeps going right at men who are a foot taller and at least 100 pounds heavier, one wonders.

Yet Iverson always got up. At 6-feet, 165 pounds, he was the smallest player on the court, but no one played with more heart. He ran the option offense for his high school football team, which meant he got hit almost every play. Iverson raced into the NBA paint like he was still playing quarterback, only without pads.

Drive the lane. Attack the rim. Go flying. Hit the floor. Bounce up. Shoot free throws. Repeat.

"He loves getting hit, but he's always been able to get back up," said former Philadelphia 76ers coach Maurice Cheeks. "It seems as though when he gets hit the hardest, he comes back and fights even harder."

Though the fearless drives are what fans remember, Iverson did most of his damage from the outside. Coming off a screen, he would stop and pop from anywhere on the floor, or he would create his own shot. He found a way to get his points, and a lot of them. Iverson's four scoring titles are exceeded only by Michael Jordan and Wilt Chamberlain. He is the shortest player ever to lead the NBA in scoring.

Iverson also is the shortest player to be picked first overall, by Philadelphia in the 1996 NBA Draft. He won the 2000-01 NBA MVP Award, the same year he led the Sixers to the NBA Finals. His regular-season average of 26.7 points per game ranked sixth in NBA history through the 2011-12 season, and his playoff average of 29.7 points per game trailed only Jordan.

LeBron James received a lot of criticism after the Miami Heat lost to the Dallas Mavericks in the 2011 NBA Finals. Though such scrutiny comes with the territory of being the best basketball player in the world, it still stung.

"It took me to go all the way to the top and then hit rock bottom basically to realize what I needed to do as a professional athlete and as a person," James said after Miami defeated Oklahoma City 4-1 in the 2012 NBA Finals. "I'm just happy that I was able to be put back in this position. I trusted my instincts, I trusted my habits that I built over the years and I just got back to being myself. And I didn't care too much what anyone said about me."

"Being myself" meant taking the Heat on his back and carrying them at times during an amazing postseason run. James averaged 30.3 points, 9.7 rebounds, 5.6 assists and 1.9 steals per game during the 2012 NBA Playoffs to join Larry Bird and Charles Barkley as the only players since 1985 to amass 600 points, 200 rebounds and 100 assists in one postseason.

"I think everything changes," said former NBA great Magic Johnson. "He can now feel that, 'I am the best player in the world because I won a ring. The ring says so. Not the media, not the marketing, but my game actually says so.' And we're judged by championships."

Nobody expects James to stop at one title, either. The 6-foot-8 star is already unstoppable, but promises to get even better.

"I've thought about what I'm going to do personally to improve my game," James said after the 2012 NBA Finals. "I always love the offseason. I'll have the opportunity to come back with something new."

Though Dennis Johnson played a key role on three NBA championship teams, he was largely unheralded and underrated during and after his career. But his teammates knew different.

"I've been very fortunate to play with Hall of Fame players," said Boston Celtics great Larry Bird. "I've played with some great ones, but DJ is *the* best player I ever played with."

That Johnson had any kind of NBA career — much less a great one — is remarkable. One of 16 children, he barely played in high school and went to work as a forklift operator after graduating. But he sprouted half a foot during a short time, attracting the attention of a junior-college coach. Johnson took off from there.

The 6-foot-4 Johnson went on to play 14 seasons in the NBA, with Seattle (1976-1980), Phoenix (1980-1983) and Boston (1983-1990). He was one of the best perimeter defenders ever, and certainly the most versatile, as he was able to slow down guards as divergent as 6-foot-1 Isiah Thomas and 6-foot-9 Magic Johnson. He was a streaky shooter who regularly caught fire in the postseason.

"He was a big-game player," Bird told the *Boston Globe*. "He always shot better in the playoffs and he always took it hard to the hole in big games."

Johnson's versatility extended to offense. In Seattle, where he played mostly shooting guard, he received the NBA Finals MVP Award after helping the Sonics win the 1979 championship. Johnson played point guard in Boston, helping the Celtics reach four consecutive NBA Finals (1984-1987), with titles in 1984 and 1986. He and Bird always seemed to be on the same page.

"We never needed any conversation on the court," Bird said in 2010, when Johnson was posthumously inducted into the Hall of Fame. "No need for talking. He just always knew what we needed."

On May 16, 1980, 20-year-old Earvin "Magic" Johnson put together one of the greatest performances in NBA history. The rookie guard, subbing for an injured Kareem Abdul-Jabbar at center, tallied 42 points, 15 rebounds and seven assists to lead the Los Angeles Lakers to a 123-107 victory over the Philadelphia 76ers in Game 6 of the NBA Finals in Philadelphia. Most of the nation, however, missed it, as only a handful of cities received the live telecast.

That was about to change. "Showtime" had arrived, with Magic playing the lead, and the NBA was about to go prime time. His brilliant play and engaging personality made him a superstar, while his cross-country rivalry with the Boston Celtics' Larry Bird brought an entire generation of fans to the NBA.

The 6-foot-9 Johnson was the tallest — and the best — point guard in NBA history. He revolutionized the game with his passing, leading a fast break that made the Lakers the hottest ticket in Hollywood. As Abdul-Jabbar grew older, Magic took on more of the scoring load while still dishing to teammates. He did it all with youthful exuberance, though beneath that smile lurked one of the NBA's most competitive players.

"I remember thinking, 'How does Magic keep up that intensity?'" said Michael Cooper, who played 11 seasons with Johnson. "He went all out all the time. He never stopped. He practiced like he played. He treated a January regular-season game like Game 7 of the NBA Finals."

Johnson led the Lakers to five NBA titles during the 1980s. He made nine appearances in the NBA Finals, won three NBA MVP Awards, and his career average of 11.2 assists per game is the highest ever.

Magic has been equally successful off the court, building a business empire. He is as popular as ever, especially in Los Angeles, where he headed the partnership that purchased the L.A. Dodgers baseball team in 2012.

"You didn't call 'bank'!" That refrain is heard on the playground whenever a shot hits the backboard and goes in, as if it was an accident and therefore should not count. Sam Jones never needed to call "bank," because when he shot, it was understood.

"I perfected [my bank shot] so well that it was like making a layup," Jones said in 2011. "Fifteen feet and in was like me making a layup because I had so much confidence in my shot. It was something new that I also brought to the NBA. It became Sam Jones' shot because I shot it so well."

Jones played an instrumental if unsung role in the Boston dynasty, helping the Celtics win 10 championships in his 12 seasons (1957-1969) with the club. The ultimate team player, he did whatever was needed to win. The 6-foot-4 Jones had speed and leaping ability, and his constant movement without the ball helped the Celtics' offense hum.

"He'll do anything you ask him," said Celtics coach Red Auerbach. "He's always in shape and ready to play, and nobody works any harder at basketball than he does."

Jones scored 17.7 points per game during his career, highlighted by a career-high average of 25.9 points per game in 1964-65. More important than quantity was quality. No Celtics player delivered more in the clutch. In 1962 alone, he made the game-winning shot in Game 7 of the Eastern Division Finals, and then in Game 7 of the NBA Finals, he scored 27 points — including 5 in overtime — to lift the Celtics over the Los Angeles Lakers.

At a Boston Garden ceremony honoring Jones after his retirement, Auerbach paid him the ultimate compliment, saying, "I would like to thank Sam Jones for making me a helluva coach."

"**D**on't be in a rush to find the next Michael Jordan. There's not going to be a next Michael Jordan."

Jordan himself uttered those words at his Hall of Fame induction in 2009, not as a boast but merely as a matter of fact. There is little debate that he is the greatest player in NBA history. The only question is whether Jordan or Muhammad Ali was the greatest athlete of the 20th century.

Like Ali, Jordan transcended his sport and became a global icon. His appeal extended to every corner of the planet, to people who didn't know a pick-and-roll from a give-and-go. What separated the 6-foot-6 Jordan from the pack was his drive to be the best, his will to win, his determination to overcome all opponents and obstacles. "Air Jordan" could do anything on a basketball court, but most of all, he could impose his will.

"The thing about Michael is he takes nothing about his game for granted," said former Chicago Bulls coach Phil Jackson. "When he first came into the league in 1984, he was primarily a penetrator. His outside shooting wasn't up to pro standards. So he put in his gym time in the offseason, shooting hundreds of shots each day. Eventually, he became a deadly 3-point shooter."

Jordan, who played 15 seasons between 1984 and 2003, led Chicago to six NBA titles and won five NBA MVP Awards. He holds NBA records for highest career scoring average (30.1 points per game) and most scoring titles (10). But Jordan's vast record collection only hints at his impact.

"Watching Michael play was like watching Babe Ruth play," Bulls chairman Jerry Reinsdorf said in 2009. "Ruth was by far the greatest player of his era...[and like Ruth], the separation between Michael and the next best player was enormous. He was a major part of people's lives."

JASON KIDD

As the Dallas Mavericks prepared to play the Miami Heat in the 2011 NBA Finals, Jason Kidd reflected.

"It's been a long journey," said Kidd, who was playing in his 17th NBA season. "We all expected things to happen a little bit quicker...but patience is one thing and also just understanding the game of basketball can be very nice and also cruel at the same time."

At age 38, Kidd became the oldest person to ever start at guard in an NBA Finals game. After helping the Mavericks defeat the Heat 4 games to 2, Kidd finally had a championship, a well-deserved honor for one of the NBA's greatest point guards.

Throughout his career, the 6-foot-4 Kidd has been able to dominate games without scoring a lot of points. Though he can put the ball in the net, he mostly sets up teammates for buckets. Kidd's peripheral vision is legendary, a handy tool at all times but especially when he is leading the break or intercepting a pass. Scorers love playing with him because he delivers perfect passes in their favorite spots.

But Kidd is not merely a fancy passer, offering a complete game on both ends of the floor plus locker-room leadership. He tops all active players in triple-doubles (107 through 2011-12), and during crucial stretches of the 2011 NBA Playoffs, the Mavericks had Kidd defend Kobe Bryant, Kevin Durant and LeBron James.

"You can't teach the stuff he does," Mavericks guard Jason Terry said during the 2011 Western Conference Finals. "His game will never ever show up [entirely] on the stat sheet. The loose balls he comes up with, the way he strips guys, the way he makes whatever play we need. When it's the fourth quarter and he's on the court, we just feel like we're going to find a way to win."

Bob Lanier played 14 seasons in the NBA, tallied 19,248 points and 9,698 rebounds, and more than held his own against some of the NBA's greatest big men. But none of it came easy.

As a youngster, Lanier was so uncoordinated that he couldn't make his grammar school team. Self-conscious about his height and big feet (he would eventually require size 22 shoes), but determined to prove himself, he joined a Boys Club team and worked out endlessly. Lanier developed into an all-city player in Buffalo and earned a scholarship to St. Bonaventure, where he led the Bonnies to the 1970 NCAA Final Four before a knee injury knocked him out and ended their title hopes.

Injuries and bad luck would plague Lanier's NBA career as well, causing him to miss considerable playing time. Early play-off exits were the norm, first in Detroit (1970-1980) and then in Milwaukee (1980-84). His deepest playoff run came in his last season, when the Bucks lost in the Eastern Conference Finals. Despite all the pain, Lanier kept battling, earning the respect of his fellow players, who elected him head of their union.

"I always admired him because he comes to play with injuries," former Pistons guard Chris Ford told the *Detroit Free Press*. "He's a guy who'd do anything to win. He's never been with a winner, unfortunately, but he is a winner."

Lanier's signature shot was a left-handed hook, and he also had a nice touch on midrange jumpers. The 6-foot-11 center displayed athleticism that belied his size, a point of pride for a player who had been told at age 11 that he would never be an athlete because his feet were too big.

Since retiring as a player, Lanier has been a successful businessman, written children's books, led several educational initiatives, and worked as special assistant to the NBA commissioner.

JERRYLUCAS

The New York Knicks, already one of the smartest teams in the NBA, got even smarter when they acquired "Dr. Memory."

Jerry Lucas, the 6-foot-8 forward and center with the photographic memory and the rainbow shot, played three seasons for New York. He helped the Knicks reach two NBA Finals, highlighted by a 1973 victory that made Lucas the first person to win championships at the high school, college, pro and Olympic levels.

"What I remember most about that year is that I thought we were the smartest team ever assembled," Lucas told the *New York Daily News* in 2003. "Not only from a basic intelligence standpoint but also from our knowledge of the game."

Before Lucas became famous as a best-selling author and began performing memory tricks on talk shows, he was Ohio's "Mr. Basketball." He was one of the greatest high school players ever, leading Middletown to two Ohio state titles and a 78-6 record in three seasons. In 1960, he was the leading scorer for Ohio State, which won the NCAA title, and the U.S. Olympic team, which captured the gold medal in Rome. He played the first six and a half seasons for the Cincinnati Royals, followed by a season and a half with the San Francisco Warriors, before coming to the Knicks in a trade.

Lucas posted amazing rebounding numbers, especially considering the fact that he was neither the tallest nor the strongest player. Careful study, he said, allowed him to anticipate where missed shots would go. Whatever his secret, he averaged 15.6 rebounds per game during his 11-season career, and he is one of only four players in NBA history to average at least 20 points and 20 rebounds per game for an entire season — and Lucas did it twice. He proved so accurate with his high-arcing 20-foot shot that it was nicknamed the "Lucas Layup."

KARL MALONE

During Karl Malone's 18 seasons in Utah, Jerry Sloan served on the Jazz staff, first as an assistant and for most of that time as head coach. Watching Malone, then a rookie, work out relentlessly, Sloan asked him, "When are you going to change?"

"He told me, 'Coach, I'll never change,'" Sloan said, "and he never did."

The model of consistency, the 6-foot-9 Malone sported a chiseled physique and a complete game throughout his 19 NBA seasons (1985-2004; he played his last season with the Los Angeles Lakers). He put the "power" in power forward, but he also had a deadly jump shot and an explosive first step to the hoop. He handled the ball, ran the floor, rebounded, played defense — in other words, he did whatever Sloan asked, and then some. Malone was rugged and amazingly durable, missing just 10 games in his Jazz career.

Malone spent that Jazz career partnered with another Hall of Fame player, guard John Stockton. The pick-and-roll is almost as old as basketball, but Malone and Stockton took it to a new level. Their versatility and high basketball IQ created so many options that opponents, even knowing the pick-and-roll was coming, could not deny an open shot. "Stockton to Malone" helped make the Jazz a perennial playoff team, including back-to-back trips to the NBA Finals.

Nicknamed "The Mailman" because of his reliability, Malone retired with 36,928 points, second only to Kareem Abdul-Jabbar (38,387) on the NBA's all-time list. He set an NBA record by tallying 12 seasons with 2,000 or more points, and his 11 All-NBA First Team selections are the most in league history.

"Karl Malone, he made himself a Hall of Fame player," said Sloan. "Karl Malone helped Karl Malone, and that's the thing that has always amazed me. He changed his body. He did all the things to try to make himself better."

When he was a teenager, Moses Malone participated in a summer basketball camp. While everybody ate lunch, he stayed on the court to practice. Time after time, he would tip the ball into the air and go up after it. Dick Vitale, a college coach at the camp who has since become better known as a television commentator, asked Malone why he did that.

"Coach," said Malone, "you got to get it before you can shoot it."

Malone went and got it like no player in NBA history. At 6-foot-10, he conceded several inches to most centers. But he conceded nothing in terms of determination and tenacity. Malone used his strength and understanding of the game to get position underneath, and then it was lights out. Either he would take a pass and score, or he would follow up a teammate's miss with a rim-shaking dunk. Desperate opponents tried fouling him, but Malone made 76.9 percent of his attempts from the charity stripe for a career total of 8,531 free throws, which was an NBA record when he retired. His total of 27,409 points still ranked seventh on the NBA's all-time list in 2012.

"Even if things weren't going right, you always knew, 'Well, we can depend on Moses. Because every night he's gonna put it back in and get to the free-throw line.' That was reassuring," said Bobby Jones, who played with Malone in Philadelphia.

Malone played 21 pro seasons (1974-1995), the last 19 in the NBA. He won three NBA MVP Awards, highlighted by the 1982-83 season, when he led a dominant Sixers team to the NBA title. He was such a savvy player that despite all the power he regularly displayed, he rarely got into foul trouble. He played his last 1,212 NBA games without fouling out, a record streak.

"Pistol Pete" Maravich, so named because he could shoot a basketball from his hip, averaged 44.2 points per game during a record-setting career at Louisiana State. He rained in shots from everywhere, so imagine his numbers if there had been 3-pointers back then. Ditto for the NBA, where he scored 24.2 points per game in 10 seasons (1970-1980).

Impressive, but that's not what everybody remembers most about the kid with the unruly hair and the baggy socks. The 6-foot-5 Maravich was, quite simply, the greatest ball-handler ever. As a passer and as a dribbler, he did things with the ball that defied belief.

"Some guys break the laws of gravity," said Boston Celtics President Red Auerbach. "This guy breaks the laws of physics."

Unfortunately for Maravich, he was a decade early. He had many fans, including Magic Johnson, who described Maravich as "the real Showtime." But unlike Johnson, who was celebrated for such showmanship during the 1980s, Pistol Pete was pilloried. Playing for mediocre teams that needed him to shoot, Maravich never had the chance to show that entertaining basketball and winning basketball were not mutually exclusive.

Maravich scored a league-leading 31.1 points in 1976-77 with New Orleans, but knee injuries would rob him of his speed and leaping ability and force him to retire. After his stunning death at age 40 during a pickup game in 1988, doctors discovered that he had a congenital heart defect, and marveled that he had survived his teen years let alone gone on to become a superstar athlete. The basketball world simply mourned.

"This guy read the court better than anybody I've ever seen," former LSU coach Dale Brown told the *Florida Times-Union* in 2011. "He had eyes where people don't have eyes. He did things with a basketball I've never seen anyone else do. He did things I didn't think were humanly possible."

Bob McAdoo could always score, thanks to a jump shot among the best the game has ever seen. Victories and respect proved more elusive.

In addition to his deadly outside shot, the 6-foot-9 McAdoo possessed great timing and athletic ability, which allowed him to block shots and dominate the boards. McAdoo started fast, racking up three scoring crowns, the 1972-73 NBA Rookie of the Year Award and the 1974-75 NBA MVP Award (34.5 points and 14.1 rebounds per game) in his first four seasons.

After that, however, McAdoo became a gun for hire. He made four NBA stops in the next five seasons, leaving hard feelings and whispers about his attitude. His production declined, and a contract dispute with the New Jersey Nets seemed to signal the end. But on Christmas Eve 1981, the Los Angeles Lakers acquired McAdoo, and he proceeded to rewrite his NBA story.

Serving as the Lakers' sixth man, a role few thought he would accept, McAdoo helped Los Angeles advance to four consecutive NBA Finals, winning in 1982 and 1985. He gave the Lakers a spark off the bench while playing defense, rebounding and doing whatever coach Pat Riley asked.

"This is the happiest moment of my life," McAdoo said after he scored 16 points to help the Lakers win Game 6 of the 1982 NBA Finals and clinch the series. "People have said bad things about me during my career, but this makes up for it. I always said I would trade my scoring titles to be on a championship team, but I guess that wasn't necessary."

McAdoo finished his NBA career by playing one season (1985-86) with the Philadelphia 76ers before going overseas to play six seasons in Italy. In 1995, Riley hired him as an assistant coach in Miami, where he works with the Heat's big men and shooters of all sizes.

Growing up in Hibbing, Minnesota, Kevin McHale remembers the day basketball became his favorite sport.

"When I went to the local sports store and asked for a pair of size 13 skates, the guy gave me a kind of funny look," said McHale, who was already 6-foot-5 and about to start high school. "It was right about then that I decided maybe I should just ask for sneakers."

Plus it was a lot warmer in the gym than it was out on a frozen lake. Hockey's loss proved to be a huge gain for basketball, as McHale would go on to develop into one of the NBA's greatest low-post players.

"He was totally unstoppable because of his quickness, diversification of moves and the long arms that gave him an angle to release the ball over a taller man or more explosive jumper," said long-time NBA coach Hubie Brown.

The 6-foot-10 McHale played 13 seasons (1980-1993), all with Boston. He joined with center Robert Parish and forward Larry Bird to form probably the greatest front line in NBA history. The trio led the Celtics to five NBA Finals, winning in 1981, 1984 and 1986. McHale averaged 17.9 points and 7.3 rebounds per game, and posted a career field-goal percentage of .554, which ranked 13th in NBA history through 2011-12. He was capable of scoring much more, as he showed in 1985 when he set a Celtics' record by scoring 56 points in a game (Bird broke the mark nine days later). But that wasn't his role.

"I never really thought about my own game," McHale said when he was inducted into the Hall of Fame in 1999. "I thought about going out there and doing what I had to do.

"You almost feel embarrassed being honored for something you had so much fun doing."

"Geo Mikan vs. Knicks."

So read the marquee at Madison Square Garden in 1949. The Minneapolis Lakers were basketball's best team, but the fans only had eyes for George Mikan.

The bespectacled 6-foot-10 Mikan was an unlikely revolutionary. Before him, guards owned the game, and big men (Mikan included) were too ungainly to have an impact. DePaul coach Ray Meyer, who created a series of drills to improve Mikan's coordination, did not have high hopes for his freshman, saying, "We just wanted him to go into a corner and get lost."

But Meyer underestimated Mikan's determination. He worked incessantly and invented several exercises of his own, including the "George Mikan Drill," which today is a part of Basketball 101. Mikan alternated hands while making layups, then moved farther away from the basket, all in constant motion from side to side, at least 200 attempts per hand.

Mikan progressed rapidly to become the first dominant big man. He led the nation in scoring each of his last two years at DePaul while averaging more than 23 points per game. On defense, he knocked so many shots out of the hoop that the NCAA banned goaltending.

He went on to play nine pro seasons between 1946 and 1956, averaging 22.6 points per game in an era when 20-point scorers were a rarity, and becoming the NBA's first star player. Mikan led his teams to seven league titles (two in the National Basketball League and five in the NBA), and he won five league scoring crowns, usually by huge margins. The NBA tried to counter his dominance by widening the lane from 6 to 12 feet, but Mikan adjusted and the Lakers won three NBA championships after the change.

"He was a great man," Shaquille O'Neal said when Mikan died in 2005. "Without George Mikan, there'd be no me."

Reggie Miller's long-distance relationship with the basket produced more than 2,500 3-pointers, 25,279 points, and an impressive collection of last-second heroics.

"He's the best I've ever seen [at making clutch shots]," said former Indiana Pacers coach Larry Brown. "You let up on him and he kills you."

Miller shined brightest in Madison Square Garden, where he stole three playoff games. For New York Knicks fans, it was like a horror movie with sequels, the worst coming in Game 1 of the 1995 Eastern Conference Semifinals. Indiana trailed New York 105-99 with 18.7 seconds remaining, but Miller scored 8 points in 11 seconds to lift the Pacers to a 107-105 victory.

For Miller, the hostile crowds on the road energized him. Always one of the game's great trash talkers, he drove opponents to distraction while verbally sparring with fans courtside, especially in New York. He even wrote a book titled *I Love Being the Enemy*, with a foreword by filmmaker Spike Lee, a Knicks fan and frequent jousting partner. Off the court, Miller was a different person.

"You've got to be a bad guy…but I'm two different people," he said. "When I'm on the stage I'm into all of that. Away from it I have to ground myself. I'd drive myself crazy if I lived like that."

Though Miller made it look easy with his high-arcing rainbows, nobody worked harder. He carried only 190 pounds on his 6-foot-7 frame, but he lasted 18 seasons (all with Indiana, the second-longest tenure with one NBA team) because he was always the first to arrive and last to leave.

"He's the most significant [Pacers] player in the last 20 years, maybe 30, since the ABA days," Indiana President Donnie Walsh said during a ceremony to retire Miller's number in 2006. "Reggie is the one who made our transformation to the NBA real."

Earl Monroe perfected his art on the playground, and then brought it to the NBA. The game hasn't been the same since.

"I was aware that my style was different just by the fact that people called me a 'hot dog,'" Monroe said. "I wasn't aware of the fact that [this] particular style changed the game. It was just part of me and what I did and how I did it."

He invented so many moves that friends called him Thomas Edison (one of Monroe's many nicknames). Spins, twists, fade-aways, reverse layups, wondrous dribbling, off-balance circus shots, no-look dishes and behind-the-back passes were regular fare for him.

Monroe, who actually preferred soccer growing up, did not begin playing basketball regularly until age 14. Despite the late start, he was a hoops legend by age 19, when he left Philadelphia to play at Winston-Salem State. There the 6-foot-3 guard averaged 41.5 points per game as a senior, and went on to become possibly the greatest one-on-one player ever.

"He didn't know what he was going to do, so how could I?" New York Knicks guard Walt Frazier said about the challenge of defending Monroe. "He had the spin move, which was new at the time. He was the first who would post and toast, just back you inside, [and] all the herky-jerky moves."

Monroe played 13 seasons (1967-1980) in the NBA and even though he had to tone down his style (especially when he joined the Knicks), he still played with an unmatched flair that has become the standard. After four-plus seasons as a superstar in Baltimore, Monroe went to New York in a trade and accepted a lesser role for a title shot. He and Frazier teamed up to give the Knicks one of the league's top backcourts, leading the team to the 1973 NBA championship.

Chris Mullin, joking about his limited athletic ability, said he probably should have picked another sport. But all he wanted to do was play basketball, and that passion took him all the way to the Hall of Fame.

"If there was anyone who had a love affair with the game of basketball, it was Chris Mullin, and the results are there to prove it," former St. John's coach Lou Carnesecca, who has known Mullin since age 10, said in 2011. "I know there are a lot of people around the country who enjoyed watching him and a lot of people who are excited that he is now a Hall of Famer."

The 6-foot-7 Mullin possessed a feathery left-handed shot, honed in his Brooklyn backyard. He practiced relentlessly and would not be outhustled, just like his boyhood idol, John Havlicek. Mullin combined high basketball IQ and a pure jumper to become a two-time All-American selection at St. John's. "Imagine if he could run and jump!" said Carnesecca.

Mullin initially struggled in the NBA, dragged down by a several factors. Golden State Warriors coach Don Nelson helped Mullin turn his life around.

Sporting his ubiquitous flattop haircut, Mullin played 16 seasons (1985-2001) in the NBA, 13 with Golden State (he is the franchise's all-time leader with 807 games) and three with Indiana. He averaged at least 20 points per game for six consecutive seasons, joining Tim Hardaway and Mitch Richmond to form the Warriors' high-octane "Run-TMC" offense, a play on Run-DMC, the name of a popular rap group.

He also won gold medals as part of two U.S. Olympic teams — the last amateur squad in 1984 and the "Dream Team" in 1992. Mullin, Patrick Ewing and Michael Jordan are the only men to play on both teams.

In eighth grade, Steve Nash came home and told his mother that he was going to play in the NBA.

"I didn't doubt him," Jean Nash said. "Whether he'd make it or not you don't know, but I knew he was going to give it a heck of a try because he works hard for what he gets."

Nothing less than mastery would do for Nash, in every competitive activity he tried — hockey, soccer, rugby, baseball, lacrosse, tennis, juggling, chess and more — while growing up in Victoria, British Columbia. Though he loved a number of sports, basketball afforded him the best chance to live his dream.

Not that it was easy. Only one American university (Santa Clara) offered Nash a scholarship, and he spent his first two NBA seasons in Phoenix as a backup. A 1998 trade sent him to Dallas, where he emerged as a top point guard, one of the best ever at distributing the ball (he ranked fifth in total assists entering the 2012-13 season) and at making his teammates better.

Though known for leading the fast break, the 6-foot-3 Nash is every bit as effective running the halfcourt offense. He dribbles and passes equally well with either hand, breaks down defenses by weaving in and out of the key, and finds a way to get to the rim. Plus he is one of the top 3-point shooters in NBA history.

During his second stint (2004-2012) with the Suns, Nash won two NBA MVP Awards while helping Phoenix become a title contender and one of the league's most exciting teams.

"He meant everything," former Suns coach Mike D'Antoni told the *Arizona Republic* after Nash was traded to the Los Angeles Lakers in the summer of 2012. "He was the face of the Suns for eight years. It doesn't get any better than that, even off the floor in what he did for the community."

Dirk Nowitzki entered the NBA in 1998 as a curiosity, an athletic 7-footer from Germany who ran the floor and preferred the perimeter to the paint. Now he is the prototype, just as Shaquille O'Neal predicted.

"He is where the big-man game will be in four or five years," O'Neal said during the 2006 NBA Finals. "When you talk great big men, it'll be based on whether guys can play like Dirk — stepping out, shooting the three, midrange game and the low-post game. I'm going to actually let my children watch his game."

All that has come to pass, but initially Nowitzki was less of a prototype and more of a stereotype — that of a "soft" European player.

"I was strictly a jump shooter," Nowitzki said, recalling his rookie season. "When they took that away, my game was pretty much over."

Working with his personal coach every summer, Nowitzki developed into a complete player: shooter, passer, rebounder, rugged defender, penetrator and superb foul shooter (he makes nearly 90 percent of his free-throw attempts). His one-legged fadeaway makes him one of the NBA's toughest covers.

"Probably the most unstoppable shot ever is the skyhook," LeBron James said during the 2011 NBA Finals. "I guess you put Dirk second. There is no way to block a 7-footer fading away on one leg."

Nowitzki, the 2006-07 NBA MVP, answered any lingering questions with his performance in the 2011 NBA Playoffs when he averaged 27.7 points per game to lead Dallas to its first title.

"He's one of the 12 or 13 players to be a 10-time All-Star, a league MVP and a Finals MVP, so that puts him in the top 12 or 13," Dallas coach Rick Carlisle said in 2012. "I don't think that can be disputed. He's had a staggeringly awesome career. There's no debate now, he's up there."

"**Y**ou should play basketball."

Hakeem Olajuwon heard people say that a lot while growing up in Lagos, Nigeria, and not just because he was tall. Anyone who had seen him play soccer or team handball knew he possessed tremendous athletic ability.

Olajuwon finally gave hoops a try at age 17, and he proved to be a quick study. Within weeks he was playing in tournaments, and though all he could do was "dunk and block shots," he soon found himself playing for the University of Houston. Then he grew to 7 feet and became "The Dream," helping the Cougars advance to three consecutive berths in the NCAA Final Four.

Another Houston team — the NBA's Rockets — selected Olajuwon first overall in the 1984 NBA Draft. He still blocked shots and dunked, but now he began to incorporate the moves he had learned on the soccer pitch and handball court. His explosiveness, agility and exquisite footwork made him the most complete low-post player ever, on both ends of the floor, and one of the greatest centers in NBA history.

"He was so strong and well-balanced," said San Antonio Spurs center David Robinson. "I always had pride in myself as a good defensive player and Hakeem, when he was on, was really not stoppable. He had everything from that fadeaway, fallaway jump shot on the baseline to the hook shots in the paint. You could take one thing away, but you couldn't take everything away."

Olajuwon played 18 seasons (1984-2002) in the NBA, all but the last with the Rockets, and he holds the NBA record for most blocked shots. In 1993-94, he won the NBA MVP, NBA Defensive Player of the Year and NBA Finals MVP Awards — the first player to win all those honors in the same season. He led the Rockets to back-to-back championships in 1994 and 1995.

Shaquille O'Neal was the most overpowering big man since Wilt Chamberlain, and contrary to Chamberlain's famous line that "nobody likes Goliath," almost everybody loved Shaq. He was unstoppable on the court and larger-than-life off it, the sun around which the NBA orbited for more than a decade.

When O'Neal retired in 2011 after 19 seasons, four NBA titles and countless sound bites, LeBron James Tweeted: "What a career for Shaq Diesel! The most dominating force to ever play the game. Great person to be around as well. Comedy all the time!!"

Comedy and thunderous dunks and finger-rolls and jump hooks and clever nicknames, and more dunks. One, two, even three defenders could not prevent Shaq from scoring if he established position near the basket. Fouling was the only way to stop him, and even that did not always succeed. O'Neal dunked numerous times with defenders draped over his 7-foot-1 frame.

Despite the physical beating he endured, Shaq rarely complained to the officials and rarely mixed it up with opposing centers. He earned opponents' regard and friendship even while flattening them.

"Shaquille is so physical and hard to guard. He's so active," Houston Rockets center Hakeem Olajuwon said after O'Neal, then playing for Orlando, scored 26 points against him in Game 1 of the 1995 NBA Finals. "I have a lot of respect for him. He's my toughest opponent."

O'Neal played for six different teams, charming fans in each stop with his engaging personality. He spent his most productive time in Los Angeles (1996-2004), leading the Lakers to three consecutive NBA titles (2000-02) while winning NBA Finals MVP Awards each year. His fourth NBA title was with the Miami Heat in 2006. Shaq finished with 28,596 points, which ranked sixth in NBA history at the end of the 2011-12 season.

"Shaq not only dominated the game of basketball but also dominated off the court [with] his personality. He's [one] of the greatest entertainers," Tweeted former teammate Magic Johnson.

ROBERT PARISH

Robert Parish holds the NBA records for most seasons (21) and most games (1,611). He capped his NBA career by helping the Chicago Bulls — his fourth team — win the 1997 NBA title. But "00" will be remembered most for his 14 seasons as a Boston Celtic.

Boston acquired the 7-foot-1 Parish in 1980, after being overwhelmed by the Philadelphia 76ers' front line in the Eastern Conference Finals. Celtics guard Cedric Maxwell nicknamed him "Chief" because his stoic expression reminded Maxwell of Chief Bromden from the movie "One Flew Over the Cuckoo's Nest." The nickname stuck, although it took on a different meaning as Parish became the franchise's unsung cornerstone, joining Larry Bird and Kevin McHale to lead the Celtics to NBA titles in 1981, 1984 and 1986.

"He does get overshadowed by Larry and Kevin," said Celtics coach K.C. Jones, "but he does get the job done and is strong in the hard areas — rebounding, blocking shots, defense. He has done it all."

Nobody set more picks for Bird than Parish, who would roll to the basket for a dunk or stop and pop his rainbow jumper. Despite his height, Chief was the most athletic of the three, able to defend big men at one end and then run the floor on the break. Parish was amazingly durable, having played 70 or more games in all but his last season, and always selfless.

"He didn't demand the ball. He was more of a team guy," Bird told the *Boston Globe* in 2007, when the Celtics' new "big three" of Ray Allen, Kevin Garnett and Paul Pierce were being compared to the original version. "It was about sacrificing, and Robert was a big part of that. He could have scored more points, but he cared about winning."

TONY PARKER

When Tony Parker entered the NBA in 2001, he looked young (he was only 19) and played young. He had quickness, yes, but not much of an outside shot and an often out-of-control playing style. Parker's play not only frustrated San Antonio Spurs coach Gregg Popovich, it seemed to confirm his initial impression.

"I thought he was unfocused. I thought he was too cool," Popovich told the *San Antonio Express-News* in 2012, recalling when he saw Parker in a pre-draft workout. "I thought he was soft."

Fast-forward a decade. Parker still looks young but he plays like a grizzled veteran. Long gone are the days when his jumper was so unreliable that teams dared him to shoot. Parker can knock down shots from anywhere, especially on pull-up jumpers, and he even hits the occasional trey.

The rest of his game has progressed as well. Parker still mesmerizes opponents with his silky smooth drives to the hoop, with better results. Early in Parker's career, those drives ended as often with a wild pass or an ill-advised shot as they did with an acrobatic basket. Now when he penetrates the middle and draws the defense, he swings the ball to the Spur who has the best look at the basket. He is a point guard in complete command of the game.

Parker helped San Antonio win three NBA titles during the previous decade, highlighted by his NBA Finals MVP Award in 2007. The Spurs, as part of their transition into a new era, have asked even more of Parker in recent seasons, and he has responded. He posted a career high in assists (7.7 per game) while leading the Spurs to the NBA's best record in 2011-12. He finished fifth in the balloting for the NBA MVP Award.

"He fulfilled the challenge and the expectations," Popovich said. "This has been his best year."

K obe Bryant sees himself in Chris Paul.

"He's going to fight to win, and not too many teams can deal with him," Bryant said after the Los Angeles Lakers lost to Paul and the Clippers in January 2012. "Chris Paul is really the only other guy in the league, other than [Bulls guard] Derrick Rose, who also has that competitive edge."

Paul has always had that fire, which allowed him to overcome his older brother and his brother's friends on the playground. In the pros, the 6-foot guard is still dominating the big kids, some of whom are more than a foot taller.

"You just have to be aggressive," Paul said. "That has always been the case in basketball — the person who is the most aggressive almost always wins. That's the way it's always been for me."

"CP3" is always aggressive with the ball in his hands, attacking the defense, seeing how they react, and responding accordingly. If he attracts a crowd, he passes to an open teammate. If Paul sees an opening, he bolts to the basket. He can score inside or out and deliver highlight-reel passes. His quickness makes him unstoppable one-on-one and disruptive on defense. Throw in that competitiveness and it is easy to see why many consider him the best point guard currently in the NBA.

After five seasons with New Orleans Hornets, Paul joined the L.A. Clippers in 2011 and led them to their first playoff berth since 2006. Los Angeles defeated Memphis in the first round before losing to the San Antonio Spurs in the 2012 Western Conference Semifinals. In Game 1 of the series against Memphis, the Clippers rallied from a 27-point third-quarter deficit to win. Paul, who insisted on staying in the game after all seemed lost, made two free throws in the final seconds to cap a rally that equaled the greatest fourth-quarter comeback in NBA playoff history.

G ary Payton was a great defender. Just ask him.

"I can lock up anybody," he said, and there is plenty of evidence from his 17 NBA seasons (1990-2007) to back up that assertion. Payton was named to the NBA All-Defensive First Team a record nine times in a row. That is why many rank "The Glove" as the top perimeter defender in NBA history, an aggressive ball hawk who pestered opposing guards to distraction.

Another list he tops: the NBA's all-time trash talkers. Payton went for quantity and quality. He was the Monet of smack talk.

"That's what you want — you want them to listen to it and try to take shots they're not supposed to because they're trying to prove to me that they can shut me up," Payton said in 2000.

He also brought an aggressive approach to offense, attacking the rim and trying to use his quickness to blow by defenders. Pro players quickly caught on, laying off and daring him to shoot. So he worked to develop his outside shot, and once that began to drop, the 6-foot-4 Payton became a complete point guard who averaged as much as 24.2 points and 9.0 assists per game in a season. He even became proficient from 3-point range, though his signature plays were the crossover dribble and the spin move, either of which left defenders flat-footed en route to a layup.

"His crossover is so old-fashioned," Phoenix Suns guard Stephon Marbury said at the 2003 NBA All-Star Game. "He just gets you with crazy, old-school game....He doesn't waste energy. That's why he has played for so long. He doesn't waste energy doing stupid things."

Payton, who missed just 27 games in his career, finished with 21,813 points, 8,966 assists and 2,445 steals, which ranked fourth in NBA history through the 2011-12 season. He played from 1990 to 2003 in Seattle, then had stints with Milwaukee, the L.A. Lakers and Boston before finishing his career in Miami. He helped the U.S. team win gold medals at the 1996 and 2000 Olympics, serving as co-captain of the latter squad.

The discussion of great power forwards begins with Bob Pettit. Nearly 50 years after he retired, his accomplishments still astound: 10 All-NBA First Team selections; first NBA player to score 20,000 points; two NBA MVP Awards; 10 consecutive seasons ranked in the top five in scoring and rebounding; and career averages of 26.4 points and 16.2 rebounds per game.

"Bob made 'second effort' a part of the sport's vocabulary," said Boston Celtics center Bill Russell. "He kept coming at you more than any man in the game."

The source of Pettit's drive can be traced to high school, where he was cut from the basketball team in each of his first two years.

"Probably it was a good thing that I was not good to start with," Pettit said in 2007. "I had to work very hard. I'd go home and practice two, three hours an afternoon. When I did start getting coordinated, started getting size, I was a lot further advanced than a lot of these guys who picked it up and found it easy to start."

Pettit eventually led Baton Rouge High School to the state title and then went on to score 27.4 points per game during a stellar career at Louisiana State. His arrival in the NBA coincided with the debut of the 24-second clock. The game suddenly sped up, and the 6-foot-9 Pettit possessed the ideal skill set — athleticism, strength, endurance and a variety of shots.

Pettit spent his entire career (1954-1965) with the Hawks, the first season in Milwaukee and the last 10 in St. Louis after the franchise moved. He led the Hawks to four appearances in the NBA Finals, all against the Celtics. The Hawks lost the first battle, in 1957, in a seven-game series that ranks as one of the greatest NBA Finals. St. Louis won the rematch in 1958, clinching the series in Game 6 thanks to Pettit's 50 points.

On Feb. 7, 2012, Paul Pierce surpassed Larry Bird (21,701 points) to move into second place on the Boston Celtics' all-time scoring list. Pierce finished the season — his 14th, all played in Boston — with 22,591 points, trailing only John Havlicek (26,395) in franchise annals.

"Paul's probably the best one-on-one player the Celtics ever had over their great history," Havlicek told the *Boston Globe* in 2012. "[He's] one of those players who has the uncanny ability to free himself for an open shot any time he wants to."

Such praise must bring a smile to those who knew Pierce in middle school and high school, when he lived almost in the shadow of the Forum in Los Angeles and cheered for the "Showtime" Lakers. "When I was a kid, I hated the Celtics," he said.

Now Pierce is the face of the Celtics' franchise, the successor of a proud legacy and beloved by Boston fans because of his relentless, physical style on both ends of the floor, and because of his loyalty.

"Paul had a chance to leave us when we were bad and instead of moaning that he wanted to go to a championship team, he stayed," Boston coach Doc Rivers said. "And he said, 'I simply want to be a Celtic and I trust that we're going to win a title someday.'"

That title came in 2008, when Pierce led the Celtics to victory over the Lakers. He won the NBA Finals MVP Award as Boston claimed its 17th NBA title and the first in 22 years.

"It means so much more because these are the guys, the Havliceks, the Bill Russells," Pierce said, referring to two of the Celtics' legends in attendance for the clinching victory in Game 6. "These guys started what's going on with those banners. They don't hang up any other banners but championship ones, and now I'm a part of it."

When Scottie Pippen was winning six titles with Chicago, all the sidekick comparisons were trotted out, e.g., Pippen was Robin to Michael Jordan's Batman. In today's NBA, the Bulls' dynamic duo has become the metaphor of choice whenever a team acquires a "complementary" player. But Jordan's considerable shadow obscures the fact that Pippen was one of the most versatile and unique players in NBA history, even revolutionary.

"There is basically a position named after him," said Scott Skiles, who coached Pippen in his last season. "Everybody wants a Scott Pippen-type three man. When they think of a three man, they immediately go to Pip's name. How many guys are that good that it happens that way?"

Not only was the 6-foot-7 Pippen a three (small forward), he played one (point guard), two (shooting guard) and four (power forward) as well. His long wingspan tormented shorter players and also allowed him to match up with big men. Shooting, passing, rebounding, ball-handling, defending the opponent's best player — Pippen could do anything that was asked of him.

"His greatest strength was his knowledge of how things worked on the defensive end of the floor," said former Bulls coach Phil Jackson. "Scottie was the voice of our team, figuratively and literally, as he did a lot of talking and kept our team on the same page. Because of that, he was very vital to the run that we made."

Pippen, who played 17 seasons (1987-2004), also won gold medals at the 1992 and 1996 Olympics. His basketball journey, which began as a walk-on player at Central Arkansas, culminated in his 2010 Hall of Fame induction.

"Think of all the things we do, the way we run our offense, how we attack people," Jordan said during the 1998 NBA Finals. "It couldn't happen without him. Anyone who knows basketball knows what he means to this team."

"There isn't a day in my life that people don't remind me of that game," Willis Reed said two decades later. No doubt it is still true today.

"That game" was Game 7 of the 1970 NBA Finals, one of the greatest moments in NBA history. Reed, the New York Knicks' center and winner of that season's NBA MVP Award, had missed Game 6 with a torn muscle in his leg, watching helplessly as Wilt Chamberlain had gone for 45 points and 27 rebounds to lead a Los Angeles Lakers' rout. The Knicks had no hope without their captain.

So when Reed walked out of the tunnel at Madison Square Garden for Game 7, it electrified the crowd and his teammates. The fans only got louder as he knocked down two outside jumpers to start the game. He did not score again, but his defense shut down Chamberlain, and the inspired Knicks overwhelmed the Lakers en route to a 113-99 victory.

Fittingly, the player most responsible for leading the Knicks out of the NBA desert authored the greatest moment in franchise history. Reed played 10 seasons (1964-1974) in New York, becoming the first Knick to win the NBA Rookie of the Year Award. He helped New York end its 12-year drought of playoff victories, and the Knicks went on to win titles in 1970 and 1973, with Reed garnering the NBA Finals MVP Award each time. The left-hander combined power with a fine shooting touch, especially from the top of the key, and nobody outworked the 6-foot-10 Reed. He was the perfect center for the Knicks' motion offense, and he could defend inside and out.

"There's not one other guy in the league who gives the 100 percent that Reed does every night, every game of the season, at both ends of the court," said Hawks forward Bill Bridges.

In his first five NBA seasons, Oscar Robertson played 384 games. During that stretch, he averaged 30.3 points, 10.4 rebounds and 10.6 assists per game. A triple-double is a big deal for most players. For "The Big O," it was just another day's work.

"Nobody ever called it a triple-double," Robertson said in 2012. "All I was ever thinking about was trying to do whatever I could to put my teammates into a position where I could get the maximum production out of them and me."

For Robertson, the position of maximum production often involved backing his man down and then shooting the ball one-handed, with his hand held high above his head. When opponents tried to counteract his power by putting a bigger man on the 6-foot-5 Robertson, he used his quickness to blow by the defender. Double team? Robertson beat those easily with his passes. He truly was unstoppable.

"When I look back on my career," says former Los Angeles Lakers great Jerry West, "he's the greatest I played against. Period."

Robertson played 14 seasons (1960-1974) in the NBA, the first 10 with the Cincinnati Royals. He posted astounding numbers, including a 1961-62 campaign (30.8 points, 12.5 rebounds and 11.4 assists per game) in which he became the only NBA player to average a triple-double for an entire season. But the heroics of the seemingly indefatigable Robertson were not enough for the short-handed Royals to overcome the dominant Boston Celtics teams of the 1960s.

Robertson, who played his last four seasons in Milwaukee, finally won a championship when he teamed with Kareem Abdul-Jabbar to lead the Bucks to a sweep of the Baltimore Bullets in the 1971 NBA Finals. The Big O finished with nine All-NBA First Team selections and career averages of 25.7 points, 9.5 assists and 7.5 rebounds per game.

212
LOCKER
FOX SPORTS NET NEW YORK
FOX SPORTS NET NEW YORK
SPURS
50
35

David Robinson's first experience with organized basketball did not last long. As a freshman in high school, he quit the team. He rarely got into games, and he preferred to pursue academic interests. The son of a Navy sailor, Robinson hoped to study engineering at the United States Naval Academy.

Robinson's body, however, had other ideas. He continued to sprout in high school, growing 3 inches per year to reach 6-foot-7. Robinson gave hoops another try as a senior and enjoyed it, but he didn't pursue any college basketball offers. He headed to Navy even though he was already too tall to serve aboard ship — and then he grew another 6 inches. From that unlikely beginning emerged the greatest player in Navy's history and one of the NBA's all-time greats.

As a junior, the 7-foot-1 Robinson led the nation in rebounding and set an NCAA record for most blocked shots in a season. As a senior, he averaged 28.2 points, 11.8 rebounds and 4.5 blocked shots per game to earn unanimous player of the year honors.

After serving two years in the Navy, Robinson joined the San Antonio Spurs in 1989 and played 14 seasons with them. He possessed speed, strength and agility, a rare combination for a big man, and used those traits to devastating effect. He helped the Spurs win NBA titles in 1999 and 2003, and won Rookie of the Year, MVP and Defensive Player of the Year Awards along with a scoring title.

Robinson shined even brighter off the court, donating considerable time and money to numerous charitable causes. Since 2003, the winner of the NBA Community Assist Award has received the David Robinson Plaque, which reads: "Following the standard set by NBA Legend David Robinson, who improved the community piece by piece."

During the 1950s, Red Auerbach's Boston Celtics were a fast-break team with a glaring hole in the middle.

"I had to have somebody who could get me the ball," said Auerbach, who coached Boston from 1950 to 1966.

That "somebody" was Bill Russell. At 6-foot-9 and 220 pounds, he was hardly a prototypical center. But Russell combined speed, athleticism and intelligence to dominate the game at the defensive end in a way the NBA had never seen before — or has seen since, for that matter.

His greatest impact came as a shot-blocker. The NBA did not keep track of blocked shots when Russell played, but nobody doubts that he is the all-time leader. His timing and long arms allowed him to block or alter almost any shot within reach. Rather than swat the ball into the stands, Russell would tip it to a teammate or collect the miss and then start the Celtics' fast break.

"Nobody had ever blocked shots in the pros before Russell came along," Auerbach said. "He upset everybody."

Russell joined the Celtics in 1956, after winning two NCAA titles at the University of San Francisco and a gold medal at the Summer Olympics. He led Boston to nine NBA titles in his first 10 seasons, including an unprecedented eight straight championships from 1959 to 1966. Russell became player-coach in 1966, and he led the Celtics to titles in 1968 and 1969 to become the first African-American coach to win a championship.

Russell retired in 1969 after having won 11 NBA titles in his 13 seasons, the greatest dynasty in NBA history.

"What he did couldn't be recorded in statistics. He changed the game and he made people change their offense," said former Celtics great Tom Heinsohn. "He totally revolutionized the game."

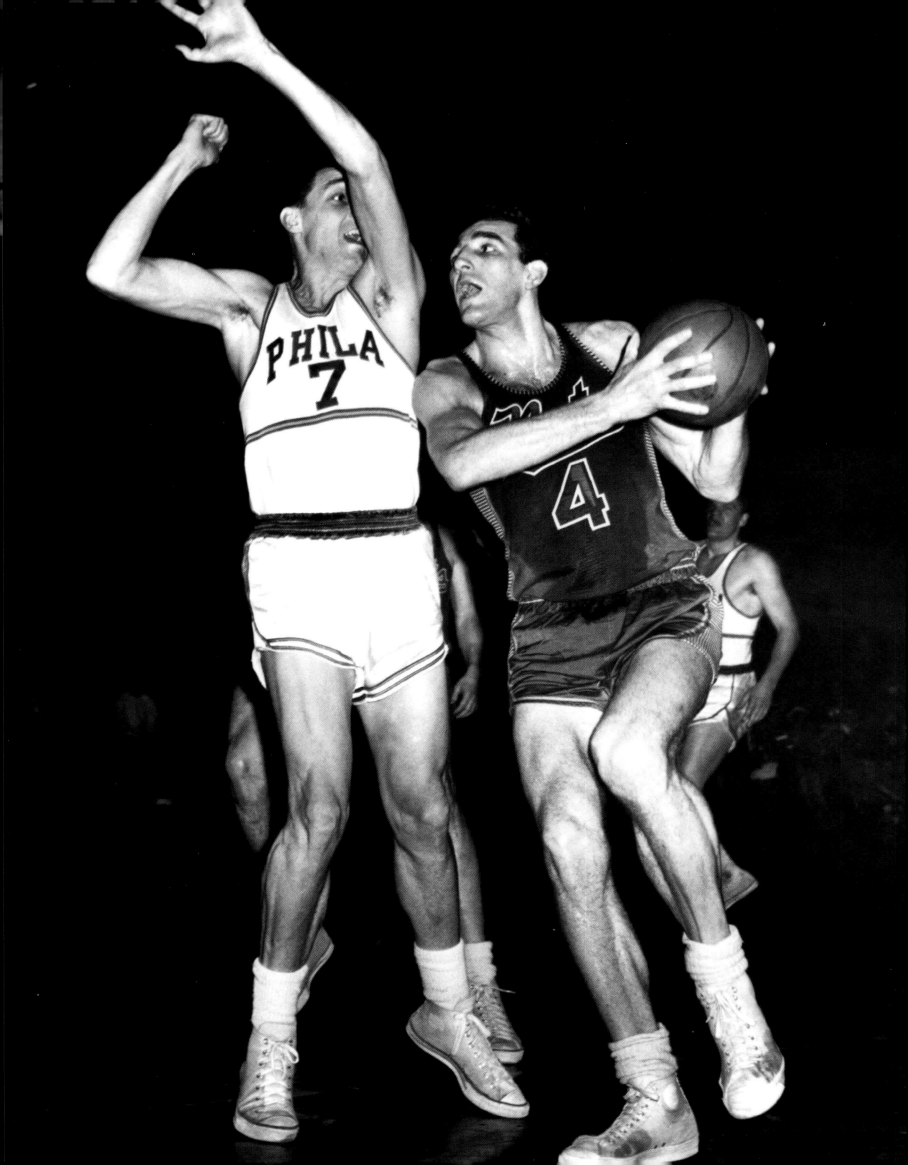

DOLPH SCHAYES

When 20-year-old Dolph Schayes graduated from New York University in 1948, he planned to play pro basketball for a year before starting his "real" career as an engineer. That year turned into a lifetime.

Pro basketball was in its infancy then, with teams valuing physicality and sharp elbows as much as skill. Schayes, who had the height (6-foot-8) but not the brawn that pro teams desired, benefited from a bidding war between the Basketball Association of America (BAA) and the National Basketball League (NBL). A year later, the leagues would merge and become the NBA, but in 1948 they were competing for players. The hometown Knicks of the BAA offered Schayes $5,000. The NBL's Syracuse Nationals offered $7,500, and Schayes accepted.

"I soon realized I didn't have the size and strength to play inside, and frankly I didn't have the pivot moves these other guys had," Schayes said. "I just felt if I kept moving it was much easier to elude my man."

Schayes practiced his outside shot for hours on end, developing an excellent perimeter game, while his constant motion kept him out of the scrum and left defenders exhausted. He proved adept at getting to the free-throw line, where he converted 84.3 percent of his attempts, and he became one of the few NBA players to make more free throws than field goals in his career.

Schayes, who led Syracuse in scoring 12 consecutive seasons, helped the Nationals win their only championship by defeating the Fort Wayne Pistons in the 1955 NBA Finals. Schayes played 16 seasons for the franchise. His last year, 1963-64, was in Philadelphia, where the Nationals moved to and became the 76ers. After retiring as a player, he coached the Sixers and the Buffalo Braves, and later served as the supervisor of officials for the NBA.

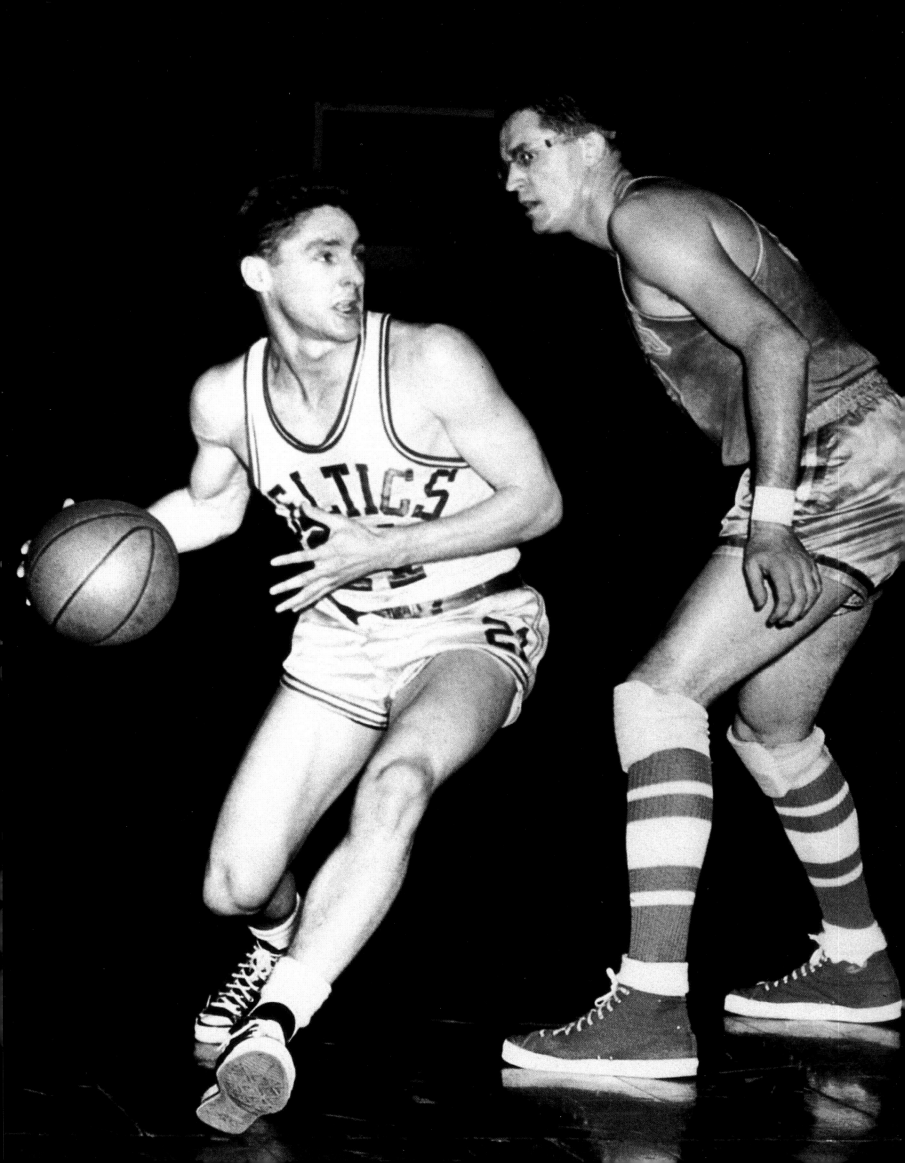

I n 1950, after graduating from USC, Bill Sharman received a call from the NBA's Washington Capitols telling him they had drafted him.

"You did? What for?" he asked. Sharman, who had signed with baseball's Brooklyn Dodgers, had not considered playing pro basketball. But when the Capitols doubled their initial offer, he figured, "Why not do both?"

So began his amazing odyssey in pro basketball. That six-decade journey has earned him 17 championship rings (as a player, coach and team executive) and two busts in the Basketball Hall of Fame (one as a player and one as a coach). John Wooden and Lenny Wilkens are the only other individuals to receive that double honor.

After the Capitols folded, Sharman played 10 seasons in Boston, joining Bob Cousy to form one the greatest backcourts ever. Cousy described Sharman as "the best athlete I've been around." Sharman harnessed that talent with countless hours of practice to become one of the greatest shooters ever.

"He was a complete technician in terms of the mechanics of the shot," Cousy said. "He never took a low-percentage shot."

Sharman also never stopped moving, whether he was trying to get open or playing tenacious defense. He led the NBA in free-throw percentage a record seven consecutive seasons, and his fierce competitiveness helped the Celtics win four championships. He also played five seasons in the Dodgers' farm system.

After retiring as a player in 1961, Sharman became a coach. He went on to become the only man to win championships and coach of the year honors in three different leagues — the American Basketball League, the ABA and the NBA. He guided the Los Angeles Lakers to a record 33-game winning streak in 1971-72, and instituted a number of innovations, including the game-day shootaround. He retired as a coach in 1976, and since has served in the Lakers' front office.

John Stockton played more seasons (19) and games (1,504) than any guard in NBA history. He sits atop the league's all-time lists for assists (15,806) and steals (3,265). During his nearly two decades in Utah (1984-2003), Stockton helped the Jazz become a perennial playoff team and advance to two NBA Finals. Yet he is still underappreciated.

Not that he would have it any other way. He eschewed endorsements and flash. There's old school, and then there's Stockton, a point guard for basketball purists. He possessed a game as fundamentally sound as anybody who ever laced up a pair of high-tops. Throw in court savvy and a lot of grit and you have the only player that legendary coach John Wooden said he would pay to see in action.

"All the time I've been around John Stockton, he's never wavered about what it takes to win," said former Jazz coach Jerry Sloan. "I don't know if we'll ever see another one like him. Not in my lifetime."

The 6-foot-1 Stockton missed just 22 games during his career, even though his 175-pound frame absorbed considerable punishment from opponents who were determined to wear him down on both ends of the court. Stockton's stamina was such that no Jazz player outlasted him during the team's conditioning drills until after he turned 40.

Most of all, Stockton was about winning, usually by distributing the ball but also by knocking down outside shots to space the court. When a new player joined the Jazz, Stockton would ask how and where he liked his passes, and then deliver the ball as requested. Such precision was possible because he practiced like he played — relentlessly and with purpose — and also with joy, albeit hidden under his impassive expression.

"I don't think anybody has that much fun playing basketball that I've ever been around," said Sloan. "He loved to play."

ISIAH THOMAS

With his beguiling smile, Isiah Thomas seemed out of place on the Detroit Pistons' "Bad Boys," who proudly played with a chip on their collective shoulder. But a fire raged underneath those pearly whites.

"Isiah was the most competitive human being I've been involved with," former Pistons assistant coach Brendan Suhr told the *Philadelphia Inquirer*. "He was a genius at his job and knew more basketball than anyone I've been around. He was consumed by the game."

Fortunately for Thomas, he was consumed by basketball rather than the mean streets of Chicago's west side, which claimed so many of his peers. He credited his mother, Mary, for protecting him from the gangs and for reining him in. No one could rein him in on the basketball court, where he was a prodigy. Thomas played at a level far above anyone else in his age group, from grade school through college at Indiana, where he led the Hoosiers to the 1981 NCAA title as a sophomore.

The 6-foot-1 Thomas went on to become arguably the greatest "small" man to play in the NBA. He could blow by any defender (the quickest player ever, according to many experts), and though he carried just 180 pounds, he was fearless in the paint. If he couldn't find an open lane, Thomas possessed a solid outside jumper, which he could knock down even with a defender in his face.

Early in his career, "Zeke" filled up the stat sheet (he averaged at least 20 points and 10 assists per game for four consecutive seasons) to turn the Pistons into a playoff team. As Detroit adopted more of a defensive mindset, Thomas sacrificed his numbers, though he still carried the team on his back when necessary. The result: three straight trips to the NBA Finals, including back-to-back titles in 1989 and 1990.

NATETHURMOND

When the San Francisco Warriors chose Nate Thurmond with the third pick in the 1963 NBA Draft, he couldn't believe it.

"I said, 'No, that can't be,' because I knew they had Wilt Chamberlain," Thurmond recalled years later.

Disbelief soon gave way to gratitude.

"What really helped my career is that every day I played against Wilt in the middle at practice," Thurmond said. "And then, when I was able to play power forward and face the basket and get a decent jump shot, it helped me in later years when Wilt was traded."

Chamberlain's departure in 1965 allowed the 6-foot-11 Thurmond to move back to center, where he became the NBA's version of a giant-killer. Both Chamberlain and Kareem Abdul-Jabbar, two of the greatest big men ever, said Thurmond was the toughest defender they faced. He also was one of the best all-around centers, notching the NBA's first official quadruple-double (22 points, 14 rebounds, 13 assists and 12 blocked shots) in 1974.

Statistics alone do not convey Thurmond's impact. His teams benefited mightily from his ability to defend opposing centers one-on-one while still protecting the rim against driving guards. On offense, Thurmond's jump shot forced his man to come out of the key, opening up the paint.

"His statistics aren't overwhelming, but his presence on the court is unbelievable," said Walt Hazzard, who played with and against Thurmond. "I've seen guys get offensive rebounds and then go back 15 feet to make sure they can get a shot off. They know Nate is there."

Thurmond played 14 seasons (1963-1977) in the NBA, the first 11 with the Warriors followed by stints with the Chicago Bulls and Cleveland Cavaliers. His average of 15.0 rebounds per game ranks fifth in NBA history, and he still holds the NBA record for most rebounds (18) in a quarter.

Only two players have won the NBA Rookie of the Year and NBA MVP Awards in the same season. Wilt Chamberlain, not surprisingly, is one. Wes Unseld is the other.

Both played center, but the comparisons end there. Chamberlain was a 7-footer who towered over the game and scored in bunches, while Unseld, generously listed at 6-foot-7, was the shortest pivot player in the NBA and preferred passing to shooting. Unseld made an impact in other ways.

Imagine running into a "block of granite," as Unseld was described. Nobody set more picks, and plowing into him was an experience not easily forgotten. His victims spent the rest of the game keeping an eye out for Unseld instead of watching the man they were supposed to defend. That block of granite proved equally impenetrable in the battle for position, controlling the glass and denying opposing centers their favorite spot on the court. He dished out punishment and outlet passes in equal doses.

"He was amazing," said teammate Phil Chenier. "He was only 6-7 but would say, 'Don't worry about the boards.' There has never been anyone better at rebounding, outlet passes and setting picks."

Unseld played 13 seasons (1968-1981) in the NBA, all with the Bullets in Baltimore and Washington. He averaged 13.8 points and 18.2 rebounds as a rookie to lead the Bullets to a 57-25 record, a 21-game improvement over the previous season. Unseld, who posted a career average of 14.0 rebounds per game, led the Bullets to the playoffs in each of his first 12 seasons, including three trips to the NBA Finals. He won the 1978 NBA Finals MVP Award while leading the Bullets to the championship.

"I didn't do anything very pretty," Unseld said. "My contributions were in the intangibles, but they were the types of things that help to lead a team."

Entering the 2003 NBA Draft, a lot of scouts didn't know what to make of Dwyane Wade. He was a "tweener," not tall enough to play small forward but seemingly not a good enough shooter to play in the backcourt. Pat Riley had a simple answer to such questions.

"He's a player," said the Miami Heat president after Miami surprised many by selecting Wade with the fifth pick. "He's a complete player who can get better."

That proved to be an understatement. Lightning quick, the 6-foot-4 Wade had an explosive first step and a 39-inch vertical leap. He was such a blur on the court that Heat teammate Shaquille O'Neal nicknamed him "Flash." Per Riley's prediction, Wade was a complete player who only got better on both ends of the floor, quickly emerging as Miami's leader and one of the NBA's brightest stars.

Wade helped the Heat improve by 17 games in his first season, followed by trips to the 2005 Eastern Conference Finals and the 2006 NBA Finals. Wade rallied Miami from a 2-0 deficit to a 4-2 series win in the 2006 NBA Finals by scoring 34.7 points per game.

Injuries slowed Wade for two seasons, but he bounced back in 2008-09 to average a career-high 30.2 points per game. In 2010, Wade found new running mates when he hooked up with a pair picked ahead of him in the 2003 NBA Draft: LeBron James, who was chosen first, and Chris Bosh, who went fourth. The trio returned Miami to title contention, a dream realized when the Heat defeated the Oklahoma City Thunder 4-1 in the 2012 NBA Finals.

"Winning the championship in 2006 was amazing, but I didn't go through nothing yet," Wade said. "Now six years after that, I've been through a lot...and this means so much more."

BILLWALTON

Bill Walton played just 468 NBA games, yet he is considered among the league's great centers. Imagine what he might have accomplished if his body had cooperated.

"He could do everything," said Jack Ramsay, Walton's coach in Portland. "He could score, rebound, block shots and run the floor. He was a great defender, and he was the best outlet passer I ever saw. If he could have stayed healthy, he probably would have been the greatest center of all time."

According to many, Walton already holds that lofty status among collegiate centers. He led UCLA to two NCAA titles, garnered national player of the year honors in all three varsity seasons, and authored one of the greatest performances in basketball history — 44 points on 21-of-22 shooting — in the 1973 NCAA Championship Game.

He barely played half of Portland's games in five seasons, but like a supernova, his brief time was brilliant. Walton and the "Rip City" Blazers rallied from a 2-0 deficit in the 1977 NBA Finals to win four straight games and stun the Philadelphia 76ers. The next season, Portland started 50-10 until a recurring foot injury sidelined Walton. He still won the 1977-78 NBA MVP Award but he was done as a full-time player.

During the 1980s, Walton excelled coming off the bench in between numerous stints on the injured list. He received the 1985-86 NBA Sixth Man Award while helping the Boston Celtics win the championship, but he played just 10 more games following that season.

After his playing career ended, Walton became a broadcaster, a gratifying achievement for a man who had been afflicted by stuttering until age 28.

"It's the greatest accomplishment in my life, learning how to speak," the often outspoken Walton said in 2012. "Now they're scouring the earth trying to find the person who can get me to stop talking."

JERRY WEST

The title of Jerry West's 2011 autobiography, *West by West: My Charmed, Tormented Life*, speaks volumes. His torment came from an abusive father and lifelong battles with insecurity and depression. The charmed part has been a career as a player and team executive that almost certainly will never be surpassed.

West escaped his unhappy childhood by shooting hoops alone in a neighbor's yard. There he developed some of the fastest hands and the quickest release the game has ever seen. He went on to star at West Virginia and help the U.S. win a gold medal at the 1960 Olympics before joining the Los Angeles Lakers.

A bundle of nervous energy on the court, the 6-foot-3 West often played past the point of exhaustion. He was unstoppable on offense, disruptive on defense and supremely confident, especially at crunch time. He was "Mr. Clutch."

"I learned that no matter what happens in a game, the last four minutes decide it," West said. "So when it comes, I'm ready."

West played 14 seasons (1960-1974), all with Los Angeles, and averaged 20 points or more per game in all but his rookie campaign. His career average of 27.0 points per game ranked fifth in NBA history through the 2011-12 season.

Championships, which had been a source of frustration for West as a player (the Lakers only won once in his nine trips to the NBA Finals), came in bunches after he retired. He served more than two decades in the Lakers' front office, from the "Showtime" era of the 1980s to the franchise's most recent championship teams, which West began building in 1996 by acquiring Kobe Bryant and Shaquille O'Neal.

"Please enjoy this moment because you deserve it," Magic Johnson said when the Lakers unveiled a statue of West in 2011. "Everything we did as a team, we did because of you."

Today Lenny Wilkens is known as the coach with the second-most victories (1,332) in NBA history. But well before he donned a suit and grabbed a clipboard, he was quite a player.

Growing up in Brooklyn, the most important man in Wilkens' life was Father Thomas Mannion, the parish priest. After Wilkens' father died, Mannion looked out for the youngster by trying to channel his energies "into something worthwhile." So began a lifetime in basketball.

Wilkens developed into an excellent ball-handler and defender while playing in Catholic Youth Organization games, but did not attract college recruiters because he played only half a season of high school ball. Mannion convinced Providence College to offer him a scholarship, and Wilkens went on to average 14.9 points and 7.3 assists per game in three varsity seasons.

In college and in the NBA, the 6-foot-1 Wilkens was the consummate point guard. He coolly directed the offense, scoring when necessary, but mostly distributing, making his teammates better by putting them in ideal positions for shots. He rarely betrayed his intentions, leaving opponents guessing.

"Lenny was a great pleasure to play against because he was such a challenge," said Boston Celtics guard K.C. Jones. "He kept you off-balance all the time. He never looked like he was doing anything and he'd have dozens of points and steals."

Wilkens played 15 seasons (1960-1975) in the NBA, averaging 16.5 points and 6.7 assists per game. The calm leadership he displayed on the floor made him a natural choice to become a coach, a second career that began in 1969 while he was still playing and extended until 2005. Wilkens was inducted into the Hall of Fame as a player (1989) and as a coach (1998), joining John Wooden and Bill Sharman as the only people with that double honor.

Dominique Wilkins had one of the greatest nicknames in sports. Sometimes, though, it obscured his greatness as a player.

"The Human Highlight Film" produced a massive collection of spectacular plays. He thrilled fans with his ability to play above the rim, and his dunks — especially the windmill (his favorite) and the spinning 360-degree varieties — are legendary. But this two-time winner of the NBA Slam Dunk contest brought much more to the hardwood.

He was a complete scorer who used his leaping ability to full advantage. The 6-foot-8 Wilkins could rise up and launch his jumper from anywhere on the floor, including 3-point range. In the post, he could catch the pass, spin, go up and shoot — all in one fluid motion.

Other areas of his game improved as his career progressed, but Atlanta, where he played 12 of his 15 seasons, counted on Wilkins to score. He engaged in some memorable duels, including a Game 7 shootout with Larry Bird in the 1988 Eastern Conference Semifinals. Wilkins scored 47 points on 19-of-23 shooting, but Bird (34 points) and the Celtics prevailed 118-116.

"It was like two gunfighters waiting to blink," said Celtics forward Kevin McHale. "There was one stretch [in the fourth quarter] that was as pure a form of basketball as you're ever going to see."

Wilkins, who was inducted into the Hall of Fame in 2006, ranked 11th in points (26,668) and 13th in scoring (24.8 points per game) on the NBA's all-time lists through the 2011-12 season. He holds the NBA single-game record for most free throws made (23) without a miss.

"I was so happy to see Dominique get inducted," said Hall of Famer Charles Barkley. "I always said he was the league's most underrated superstar, and he never got the credit he deserved. He carried a lot of Hawks teams on his back."

James Worthy possessed the attributes of a superstar. He had speed, quickness and size (6-foot-9), plus he could pass, defend and rebound. He had an array of post moves, and he was the best finisher at the basket since Julius Erving.

But superstardom was not for Worthy, who preferred rings to scoring crowns. He was a coaches' player, unsung and content with his role yet able to step into the spotlight when needed.

The legend of "Big Game" James began when he led North Carolina to the 1982 NCAA title. Michael Jordan's basket lifted the Tar Heels over Georgetown, but it was Worthy who was named Most Outstanding Player after scoring 28 points in the championship game on 13-of-17 shooting.

The Los Angeles Lakers selected Worthy with the first pick in the 1982 NBA Draft, bypassing flashier options for a player they thought was a better fit. The wisdom of their choice would be confirmed repeatedly during the next 12 seasons, as Worthy helped L.A. advance to seven NBA Finals, winning three. Kareem Abdul-Jabbar and Magic Johnson received more ink, but Worthy took "Showtime" to another level.

"James is the fastest man of his size in the NBA," Lakers coach Pat Riley said in 1988. "In terms of finishing the fast break creatively and swiftly and deceptively, no one else compares."

Worthy's clutch credentials included a playoff average of 21.1 points per game, nearly 4 points more than his regular-season average. He delivered one of the greatest postseason performances ever in Game 7 of the 1988 NBA Finals by tallying 36 points, 16 rebounds and 10 assists to lift Los Angeles to a 108-105 victory over Detroit. It was the only triple-double of his career, and he was named NBA Finals MVP. True to form, Worthy said he would have voted for Magic.

PASSION FOR THE GAME

What makes a great NBA player? The first thing any player needs is attitude. Attitude turns into a passion for the game. You have to love what you do, and you have to be willing to make all of the sacrifices to maximize all of your talent. Then you have to do a little extra to improve. Playing longevity is also important. You have to play through pain from time to time. It is also essential to be a good teammate.

Inside the pages of *The NBA's Greatest Players*, you will read about 75 of the best to play the pro game, all of whom fit the above description, and I am very honored to be included in that list.

During my time in the NBA with the Lakers, I was around two of the game's greatest players — Magic Johnson and Kareem Abdul-Jabbar — every day.

Magic was a great individual player who had all of the intangibles. He had the ability to make big shots and plays, and then he enhanced the game of every teammate by encouraging and inspiring by example. He was a winner by willing it to happen. He was very dedicated and committed.

Kareem brought a sense of calm and intensity at the same time. His calmness was all about preparation. We'll never see a skyhook like his again. He was able to tap into certain intangibles that a lot of others aren't able to when they are tired. He was not very vocal, but he took a scalpel to slice his way through the game and made great things possible.

If I had to choose a player to start my team, I would choose Magic. I don't know if he is the greatest player, but it would be very difficult to choose between him and Kareem because they both did the same things. But Magic even made Kareem better.

Larry Bird was another player who fit the description. He did not have a lot of athleticism, but he had the theory and the science of the game down to a "T" through a lot of hard work. Kevin McHale was a versatile and dominant player. Dennis Rodman dominated the game without scoring. Alex English was a scorer and very precise shooter. Michael Jordan had tremendous drive and learned from his defeats in his rise to the top. Clyde Drexler and Hakeem Olajuwon were impact players.

Among today's players, I am a huge Kevin Durant fan. His attitude is tremendous, and he continues to get better. LeBron James has emerged as a mature player who knows how to be great, when to make good decisions and when to take over the game. Kobe Bryant has demonstrated all of those traits over his tenure with the Lakers. Dirk Nowitzki is as solid as they come. Tim Duncan is not flashy, but very effective. All of those guys could have played in the 1980s, and all have certainly earned a place in this book.

— *James Worthy,*
Los Angeles Lakers, 1982-1994

About the Author

John Fawaz has contributed to numerous sports publications as both a writer and editor, including *The Official NBA Encyclopedia*, the *NBA Finals Program*, *NFL's Greatest* and the *Super Bowl Game Program*. He began his career in the sports department of the *Los Angeles Times* and later served as managing editor of the NFL's Creative Services division.

Acknowledgments

Many thanks to the staff at Whitman Publishing, and to my collaborator on all things great and small, my wife Joycelyn.

Photo Credits

All photographs appearing in this book are credited to NBA Entertainment/Getty Images.